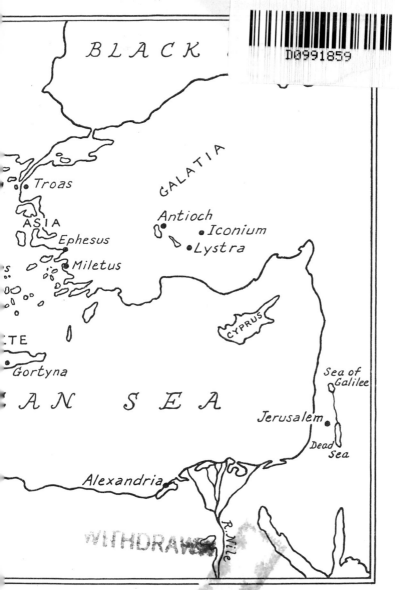

BLACK

GALATIA

Troas

ASIA

Antioch

Iconium

Ephesus

Lystra

Miletus

CYPRUS

TE

Sea of
Galilee

Gortyna

Jerusalem

AN   SEA

Dead
Sea

Alexandria

R. Nile

TERRANEAN

THE NEW CLARENDON BIBLE
(NEW TESTAMENT)
General Editor: THE REV. H. F. D. SPARKS, D.D., F.B.A.

THE PASTORAL EPISTLES

Codex Sinaiticus, showing (top left-hand corner) 1 Tim. 3:16, with the reading 'he who' (ὅς) corrected to 'God' (Θεός).

The Pastoral Epistles

IN THE NEW ENGLISH BIBLE

With introduction and commentary

by

C. K. BARRETT, D.D., F.B.A.

PROFESSOR OF DIVINITY IN THE
UNIVERSITY OF DURHAM

OXFORD

AT THE CLARENDON PRESS

1963

Oxford University Press, Amen House, London E.C.4

GLASGOW NEW YORK TORONTO MELBOURNE WELLINGTON
BOMBAY CALCUTTA MADRAS KARACHI LAHORE DACCA
CAPE TOWN SALISBURY NAIROBI IBADAN ACCRA
KUALA LUMPUR HONG KONG

PRINTED IN GREAT BRITAIN
AT THE UNIVERSITY PRESS, OXFORD
BY VIVIAN RIDLER
PRINTER TO THE UNIVERSITY

GENERAL EDITOR'S PREFACE

THE success of the New Testament volumes of the Clarendon Bible series, based on the Revised Version, has prompted its publishers to think that the public will welcome a similar series, of comparable level and plan, based on the text of the New English Bible. Like its predecessor, therefore, the New Clarendon Bible (New Testament) sets out to furnish concise commentaries on individual books of the New Testament, suitable for candidates taking G.C.E. 'A' level, students in universities and teacher training colleges, and others. In commissioning volumes the policy is twofold: both to fill the gaps in the old series by covering those books which have not been covered, and also to include the other books, switching over to the *N.E.B.* text, as and when the time seems ripe and editors become available. No further volumes will therefore be added to the old series, but its volumes will be kept in print as long as there appears to be a sufficient demand for them.

The design of the new series follows that of the old, except that it has been thought more useful to print both text and notes on the same page: subjects requiring more comprehensive treatment than the scope of the notes allows will as before be found in the introduction and in appendixes at the end of each volume. It is hoped that the illustrations will be found as valuable a feature of the new series as of the old.

AUTHOR'S PREFACE

The reader of the New Testament has at his disposal a number of commentaries on the Pastoral Epistles, and all that I have read contribute something, and some contribute a great deal, to the understanding of the Epistles. Unfortunately, within the limits of a commentary in the Clarendon Bible I have been able to make very few references to a notable body of literature, but some of the most useful works will be found in the list on p. 35. Of them all, I should like to draw special attention to the commentaries by John Calvin and C. Spicq. This is not the place to mention by name those general works of reference on which every student of the New Testament constantly and gratefully relies.

I have tried to deal, as every commentator on these Epistles must, with the question of their authorship, but I remain convinced that it is a trivial issue in comparison with the task of exegesis; and I have ventured to reconstruct their historical setting in the primitive Church, without, however, giving up the belief that the context in which they should be studied is that of biblical theology. If any justification is required for a new commentary on the Pastorals these two facts may serve —together with the growing conviction, which study of the Pastorals has deepened, that much of the modern debate on the Church and the Ministry has concerned itself with trivialities instead of the fundamentals to which the unknown author of these Epistles summons us.

A second limitation has been placed upon me by the narrow space permitted to a commentator in the Clarendon Bible. I never wished to print a dedication in any book till this, and here no page is available for the purpose. I therefore simply record in this Preface that, as I have worked on these Epistles, I have constantly recalled my father—a man of God, a good minister of Jesus Christ, who laboured in the word and doctrine, did the work of an evangelist, and kept the faith.

C. K. BARRETT

Durham

CONTENTS

LIST OF ILLUSTRATIONS

INTRODUCTION

1. *The Pastoral Epistles in the New Testament Canon*

(a) *Early Allusions and Quotations*. The three epistles, 1 and 2 Timothy and Titus, were not described as 'the Pastoral Epistles' in ancient times. The term is said to have been used by Thomas Aquinas, but has become common only since the eighteenth century.

The first Christian writer who can be confidently claimed to have known the Pastorals is Polycarp, bishop of Smyrna early in the second century, who declares:

> The love of money is a source of all evils. Since then we know that we brought nothing into the world, nor have we anything to carry out . . . (Polycarp, *To the Philippians* iv. 1);

and

> They did not love the present age (ix. 2).

Cp. 1 Tim. 6:10; 6:7; 2 Tim. 4:10. The sentiments in the first passage are common-place, but it is unlikely that so much of the language of the Pastorals should be reproduced by chance.[1]

A few other passages in the Apostolic Fathers have been alleged as echoes of the Pastorals; none is convincing. Indeed, around and immediately after Polycarp silence prevails. It is especially noteworthy that Justin Martyr (c. A.D. 150), who shows traces of most of the Pauline Epistles, appears to be completely ignorant of the Pastorals, and that they are not included in the canon of the ardent, though heretical, 'Paulinist', Marcion. It is sometimes held that Marcion may have omitted the Pastorals because they were unfavourable to his theological views (by some indeed that the Pastorals were written *against* Marcion; see below, p. 13, and on 1 Tim. 6:20), but if he had edited them as freely as he edited other epistles he could in fact have made good use of them. It is therefore probable that he was simply

---

[1] H. von Campenhausen (*Polykarp von Smyrna und die Pastoralbriefe*; Sitzungsberichte der Heidelberger Akademie der Wissenschaften, Phil.-hist. Klasse, 1951) suggests that Polycarp wrote the Pastoral Epistles. This is possible, but beyond proof.

unaware of their existence. The Pastorals are not among those epistles to which there are 'Anti-Marcionite' prefaces.

Later in the second century, Irenaeus (bishop of Lugdunum, c. A.D. 178–200) quotes fairly frequently from the Pastorals, and evidently regarded them as Pauline, arguing, for example, on the basis of 2 Tim. 4:10 f. that Luke was a constant companion of Paul's (Adv. Haer. III. xiv. 1). From this time the Pastorals are regularly quoted, and used as the work of Paul, though it seems probable that they were not contained in the third-century Chester Beatty Papyrus (P[46]) of the Pauline letters; doubt has been thrown on their authorship only in the modern period of critical biblical study. Any account, however, that we may give of their origin must if possible explain the fact that up to the middle of the second century, or indeed somewhat later, they were by no means widely known, though (as the evidence of Polycarp proves) they were in existence.

(b) *Statements about the Epistles and their Origin.* The Pastoral Epistles came slowly into use, but once used they were recognized as the work of Paul, and the fact that they were addressed to private individuals did not prevent them from achieving widespread circulation and official authority. They are mentioned in the Muratorian Canon (c. A.D. 200), after reference to the other Pauline letters (including Philemon but not Hebrews), as follows:

The one [epistle] to Titus, and the two to Timothy, [were written] out of affection and love, yet have been consecrated to a position of honour in the catholic Church for the ordering of ecclesiastical discipline.

The ostensibly personal intention with which the letters were written was soon lost sight of. The author of the Muratorian Canon thinks of 'ecclesiastical discipline', having regard, no doubt, mainly to the paragraphs in the Epistles dealing with the ministry. Irenaeus, naturally enough, thought of them as part of the Church's defence against gnostic heresy. He opens his *Adversus Haereses* with an allusion to 1 Tim. 1:4 (note also the allusion to Luke 1:1–4):

Inasmuch as certain men have set the truth aside, and bring in lying words and vain genealogies, which, as the apostle says, 'minister questions rather than godly edifying which is in faith', and by means of their craftily constructed plausibilities draw away the minds of the inexperienced and take them captive . . . (*Adv. Haer.* I, Preface, 1).

Of several similar passages we may quote:

> As many as separate from the Church, and give heed to such old-wives' fables as these, are truly self-condemned; and these men Paul commands us, 'after a first and second admonition, to avoid' (*Adv. Haer.* I. xvi. 3; cp. Tit. 3:10).

The same two passages are quoted by Tertullian in *De Praescriptione Haereticorum* 7 and 6 respectively. Tertullian also can use the Pastorals 'for the ordering of ecclesiastical discipline'. The following is a characteristic passage:

> How detrimental to faith, how obstructive to holiness, second marriages are, the discipline of the Church and the prescription of the apostle declare, when he suffers not men twice married to preside, when he would not grant a widow admittance into the order unless she had been 'the wife of one man' (*Ad Uxorem* i. 7; cp. 1 Tim. 3:2; 5:9; Tit. 1:6).

Tertullian in fact has almost ceased to consider the Pastorals as personal letters, though he suggests (without ground) that it may have been for this reason that Marcion did not use them:

> I wonder, however, when he receives this letter [Philemon] which was written but to one man, that he rejected the two epistles to Timothy and the one to Titus, which all treat of ecclesiastical discipline (*Adv. Marcionem* v. 21).

Thus as early as A.D. 200 the position of the Pastorals is undisputed, and it is not surprising that Eusebius (*Historia Ecclesiastica* III. iii. 5) should describe them (with the rest of the fourteen letters of Paul) as 'well known and undisputed'. Hebrews indeed finds only qualified admission to this list of undisputed works; but not so the Pastorals.

(*c*) *The Epistles accepted as Canonical.* The Pastoral Epistles made a slow start in their progress towards canonical authority, but not a slower than other of the smaller Pauline letters. It is sometimes maintained that the Pauline corpus came to its present composition through clear-cut stages: first a ten-letter collection (letters to churches with that to Philemon, probably attached to Colossians), and then a thirteen-letter collection, consisting of the above, together with the Pastorals (Hebrews being sometimes but not always added as a fourteenth); but this is probably an undue simplification of a much more complicated process. The authorship of the Pastorals does not appear ever to have been doubted (as it must have been, had they been known by second-century authors to have been of recent origin), and no one, it seems, wished to deny them canonical status on the ground that they were addressed to individuals. It is probable that throughout the first half of the second century the Pauline Epistles were becoming better and better known, though having no thought-out and defined status. In the middle of the second century Marcion issued his *Apostolicum*, and when the Church replied with its bigger and better canon the Pastorals, so admirably suited as a counterblast to Marcion that some have thought that they were written for the purpose, were added.

2. *Authorship*

(*a*) *External Evidence*. The material collected in the previous chapter makes up the whole of such external evidence as exists for the authorship of the Pastoral Epistles. The most important feature of it is the fact that no one in antiquity appears to have doubted the Pauline origin of the letters. They seem to have been accepted by all, whether orthodox or heretical, who knew them. This fact is not in itself very significant; the Epistles bear Paul's name and purport to have been written by him, and literary criticism was not in the early centuries sufficiently advanced to question such direct attribution. Only a few questioned the Pauline authorship of Hebrews, though this bears no author's name, and when Dionysius of Alexandria felt constrained to deny that Revelation had been written by the Fourth Evangelist he ascribed it to another author of the same name—he did not question that it was, as it claimed to be, written by one called John. Once therefore the Pastorals had begun to circulate under the name of Paul, only a very strong contrary tradition, or a well-sustained charge of heresy, could have persuaded their readers that they were not what they appeared to be.

It nevertheless remains both true and significant that Pauline authorship was not questioned until comparatively modern times. The only negative bearing of external evidence upon the question of authorship must therefore be found in the comparative disuse of the Pastorals in the early second century, and here the Pastorals are in little worse case than other Pauline letters such as Colossians and 1 and 2 Thessalonians. It is, however, hard to see how Marcion could have omitted them from his list if they had been known to him as Paul's (and if they were known to him at all, he must have known them as the work of Paul), and they contain material which could hardly have failed to be congenial to Justin. To this it may be answered that private letters would naturally come before the public eye more slowly than epistles addressed to churches, and that in truth there is nothing in the external evidence that a defender of the authenticity of the Epistles needs to explain.

(b) *Linguistic Argument.* Other more serious objections to Pauline authorship arise, and the first of these must now be considered. Study of the vocabulary and style of the Pastoral Epistles reveals significant differences from the certainly genuine letters. The data may be set out as follows:

(1) The Pastoral Epistles contain a large number of words which do not occur elsewhere in the New Testament. According to Dr. P. N. Harrison (*The Problem of the Pastoral Epistles* (1921)),[1] these *hapax legomena* amount to 175 (about 20·6 per cent. of a total vocabulary of 848 words, omitting proper names), of which 96 occur in 1 Timothy, 60 in 2 Timothy, and 43 in Titus. This means that, within the New Testament, the vocabulary of the Pastorals is highly distinctive, and is so to a far greater extent than that of any one of the genuine Pauline letters. Thus Dr. Harrison calculates that whereas 1 Timothy has 15·2 *hapax legomena* per page, 2 Timothy 12·9, and Titus 16·1, Romans has only 4, and Philippians, which among the ten Pauline letters yields the highest figure, has only 6·2. If therefore Paul wrote the Pastoral Epistles he acquired a markedly fresh vocabulary for the purpose.

(2) This conclusion is reinforced if we count up the words which occur in the Pastorals and in other New Testament books, but not in any of the ten main Pauline letters. Dr. Harrison's figures are as follows: There are altogether 131 such words, of which 1 Timothy has 77, 2 Timothy 54, and Titus 38. If we add these figures to those in the previous paragraph we shall find the number of words in each of the Pastorals which have no parallel in any Pauline letter. The results are: for 1 Timothy, 173 out of a total vocabulary of 529 (1 word in 3, or 27·3 per page); for 2 Timothy, 114 out of a total of 413 (more than 1 in 4, or 24·4 per page); for Titus, 81 out of a total vocabulary

[1] See also *Journal of Theological Studies*, xlix (1948), 204–10.

of 293 (2 in 7, or 30·4 per page). These figures are evidently high, but are seen in their true light only when compared with figures drawn from other Pauline letters. Romans has 10 words per page not contained in the other nine letters; the highest figure obtained among the ten letters is again that for Philippians, but this is no more than 12·7. It thus becomes clearer than ever that if Paul wrote the Pastorals he used a new stock of words in doing so. If Pauline authorship is to be maintained some explanation of this fact will have to be found.

(3) These observations can be confirmed by working in the opposite direction. A number of characteristic Pauline words which appear fairly frequently in the ten epistles are missing from the Pastorals. The following are examples (the number of occurrences in the ten letters being given in brackets): ἀκρο-βυστία (19), ἀποθνήσκειν (42), ἐλεύθερος (16), ἐργάζεσθαι (18), εὐαγγελίζεσθαι (21), εὐχαριστεῖν (24), καυχᾶσθαι (34), οὐρανός (21), πνευματικός (24), πράσσειν (18), σοφία (28), σῶμα (91), υἱός (40), χαίρειν (29), ψυχή (13). A list of this kind can prove little, since each of the above words is missing from at least one of the ten epistles; it may, however, be suggestive, and particularly suggestive is the fact that many of the Pauline particles and similar words (and no words do more to give distinctive colour to Greek style than do the particles) are not used in the Pastorals. Such characteristic words as ἄρα, ἄρτι, διότι, εἴτε, ἐπεί, ἰδού, καθάπερ, νυνὶ δέ, οὐχί, ὥστε, are missing from the Pastorals, and it is worth while to add to these the preposition σύν, which plays an important part in Paul's thought as well as in his vocabulary.

Here are the fundamental negative data; they might be greatly expanded if we were to note Pauline phrases and constructions absent from the Pastorals, and phrases characteristic of the Pastorals (such as 'Here are words you may trust') but absent from Paul. The question that must sooner or later be answered is whether these differences between the Pastoral Epistles and the ten Pauline letters are compatible with belief in Pauline authorship or not. It is true, as defenders of the authenticity of the Pastorals always comment, that style is not static. Style is the man, and as the man grows older, enters into new circumstances and experiences, and therefore changes, so his style changes. Parallels to the statistics of *hapax legomena* are adduced from the plays of Shakespeare, and from the work of Plato. It cannot, however, be said that any of these counter-arguments is convincing, even if in addition it is urged that many of the linguistic peculiarities of the Pastorals are due to the work of a secretary to whom Paul gave considerable freedom in the drafting of the letters. For in addition to the stylistic differences there are also differences in outlook and doctrinal emphasis (which will be noted from time to time below), and if the secretary was responsible for these he was not a secretary but an author.

(4) In addition to the negative arguments based upon differences between the language of the Pastorals and that of the ten Pauline letters, a positive argument has been employed. The linguistic peculiarities of the Pastorals, which lack parallels in Paul, can be paralleled in the literature, Christian and pagan, of the second century; that is, the affinities of the Pastorals are with the Apostolic Fathers and the Apologists, rather than with the Apostles. There is some value in this argument, but not as much as in the negative arguments; for the remains, especially of Christian literature, of this period are too scanty to enable us to decide with confidence which words were current in the first century, which in the second. Nevertheless, when it is remembered that the Pastorals contain many other late features—in Church order, doctrine, discipline, and credal formulation—the second-century parallels in the realm of language also take their place in an argument that makes it difficult to accept Pauline authorship.

(c) *Historical Framework*. The question of authorship may now be approached from a different angle. If the Epistles were written by Paul, it might be expected that they could be fitted into the framework of his life as this is otherwise known. If they cannot be placed in this framework, there will be a presumption that they are not genuine. This argument, however, will fail in force so far as it is recognized that Acts does not give, and was probably not intended to give, a complete account of Paul's life. It must not be assumed that what is not mentioned in Acts cannot have occurred. In particular, it must not be assumed that Paul's life and ministry came to an end with the two-year period mentioned in Acts 28:30. This is neither stated nor necessarily implied by the text. The possibility of release, and of further travels in, it may be, both East and West cannot be excluded.

With these observations we turn to the Epistles.

1 Timothy contains little material. Only two verses suggest the circumstances in which the Epistle was written: 1:3 (When I was starting for Macedonia, I urged you to stay on at Ephesus); and 3:14 (I am hoping to come to you before long). It is suggested that Paul had recently been in Ephesus, but had left there for Macedonia, leaving Timothy behind; also that he was at liberty, able to make plans for his future movements, and within reach of Ephesus. This seems to correspond with the statement of Acts 20:1–5 (cp. 19:22), provided that in 20:5 we accept the reading προσελθόντες (instead of προελθόντες). This is a good reading (approved by J. H. Ropes, *The Beginnings of Christianity*, iii (1926), 190), and probably original, since the alternative can be accounted for as an attempt to harmonize with the data of the Corinthian correspondence. 1 Timothy can thus be fitted into Acts, but at the expense of the Corinthian letters; its position in the narrative framework can scarcely be described as secure. Indeed the evidence is too slight to warrant any decisive judgement.

In 2 Timothy the position is different. Here there is a wealth of material. Paul is able to look back upon a long career. The earliest events mentioned are the sufferings in Antioch, Iconium, and Lystra (3:11; cp. Acts 13, 14); but much has happened since then. Paul has ministered in Ephesus, where Onesiphorus helped him (1:18); possibly it was there that Alexander did him a great deal of harm (4:14; cp. Acts 19:33). If so, it may have been on this occasion that every one in the province of Asia deserted him (1:15). He has reached Rome, and been in prison there (1:17); presumably (though not certainly) it was there that he stood trial (4:16), and, it seems, was released. After this first hearing, he seems to have travelled again; he has been in Troas, where he left his cloak (4:13), and in Miletus, where he left Trophimus (4:20). We hear of other movements and dispositions, some intended by Paul (4:12, 20), others not (4:10). Now Paul is once more in prison (1:12; 2:9), and desires the presence of Timothy and of Mark (4:9, 11, 21), for he knows that this time the end is at hand (4:6 ff.).

It will be seen that these three notes, when taken together as they are presented in 2 Timothy, require the assumption that at the end of the Roman captivity described in Acts 28 Paul's case was dismissed so that he was able to resume missionary activity. This may be true, but there is no definite evidence to support it. It may be better to suppose that some of the data we have here considered were drawn from genuine Pauline fragments which have been distorted by being combined in 2 Timothy. See pp. 10 ff.

Titus presents a relatively simple situation. Titus has been left behind in Crete in order to organize churches which have, it seems, been founded in a rapid missionary tour (1:5). Paul himself is at Nicopolis, or will shortly be there (3:12). This verse and the next indicate that his assistants were moving freely, and it is clear that Paul too is at liberty, since he can make up his own mind where he will spend the winter.

Acts gives us no account of the evangelization of Crete. Acts 27:7 f. certainly afforded no opportunity, since Paul was a prisoner and the centurion in command of the party was pressing on rapidly to Rome. We must either posit a major missionary campaign passed over in silence by Acts, or place the events referred to in Titus after a supposed first hearing and release of Paul.

It thus requires ingenuity and imagination to place the Pastoral Epistles within the framework of Acts, and of Paul's ministry. A far simpler and more convincing hypothesis is that some at least of the historical notes belong to fragments of genuine epistles, but are given a false historical context by their present setting in the Pastorals.

A further point may be taken here. The picture of Timothy and Titus given in the Pastorals scarcely corresponds with that which is given by Acts and the genuine epistles. According to Acts, Timothy was called at the beginning of the second missionary journey (16:1–3), and from that time continuously accompanied and assisted Paul (17:14 f.; 18:5; 19:22; 20:4). He is named as co-writer of 2 Corinthians, Philippians, Colossians, 1 and 2 Thessalonians, and Philemon; and as a fellow-worker and fellow-preacher at Rom. 16:21; 2 Cor. 1:19. At Phil. 2:20 Paul declares that he has no assistant like him. He appears as undertaking responsible duties at 1 Cor. 4:17; 16:10; Phil. 2:19; 1 Thess. 3:2, 6, and notwithstanding 1 Cor. 16:10, which perhaps reflects some inexperience, there can be no doubt that Timothy was a trusted and efficient colleague. Now 2 Timothy at least represents itself as written considerably later than any of the Epistles just referred to; yet in it Timothy is treated as young and inexperienced. He must turn from the wayward impulses of youth (2:22), and needs to learn the first principles of Christian service (e.g. 2:3, 14; especially 2:7: 'The Lord will help you to full understanding'). Paul must remind him of his own apostleship (1:11).

Acts has no information about Titus; but references in 2 Corinthians (2:13; 7:6, 13 f.; 8:6, 16, 23; 12:18) and Galatians (2:1, 3) show that he too was a responsible, trusted, and senior assistant. In the Epistle, however, that bears his name he is given elementary instruction, and is told to make himself an example to the younger men of the church.

From these observations it seems natural to draw the conclusion that the picture of Timothy and Titus which the Pastorals give us is fictitious, founded in fact, no doubt, but not accurately representing it.

(d) Genuine Fragments. It is very difficult to think that the Pastoral Epistles were put into the shape in which we read them by Paul himself. Literary, historical, and doctrinal reasons combine to suggest this. It is, however, also true that within the Pastorals a number of fairly short passages seem, on literary, historical, and doctrinal grounds, to be thoroughly Pauline. The suggestion lies near at hand, and has been fairly widely accepted, that the author of the Pastorals incorporated in his work fragments of genuine Pauline letters. In this way, both the Pauline characteristics of certain verses, and the non-Pauline characteristics of the Epistles as a whole, receive their due. This theory will gain weight so far as the alleged Pauline fragments can be reasonably fitted into the framework of Paul's life. It will be best discussed if we work on the basis of the suggestion of Dr. P. N. Harrison,[1] who isolates five genuine fragments as follows:

(1) Titus 3:12-15. 'Paul writes from Western Macedonia, several months after 2 Cor. 10-13, and before 2 Cor. 1-9, bidding Titus, who is at Corinth, be ready to join him in Epirus' (p. 115).

(2) 2 Tim. 4:13 ff., 20, 21a. 'Paul writes from Macedonia, after the visit to Troas mentioned in 2 Cor. 2:12 f., bidding Timothy, who has returned to Ephesus, join him before winter' (p. 118).

(3) 2 Tim. 4:16-18a(?18b). 'Paul writes from Caesarea, soon after his arrival under escort from Jerusalem' (p. 121).

[1] *The Problem of the Pastoral Epistles*. See also *New Testament Studies*, ii (1956), 250-61.

(4) 2 Tim. 4:9–12, 22b. 'Timothy is recalled to Rome, *c*. A.D. 62' (p. 122). He 'has presumably been to Philippi, as promised in Phil. 2:19, 23, but instead of returning at once, has taken first the opportunity to visit his old home at Lystra' (p. 123).

(5) 2 Tim. 1:16 ff.; 3:10 f.; 4:1, 2a, 5b; 4:6 ff.; 4:18b, 19, 21b, 22a. The previous 'message reached Timothy too late . . . [Paul] breaks to him the news that they two will not meet in this world again' (p. 124).

All these passages will repay careful and detailed consideration. Here the following general observations may be made.

(1) In all the passages given by Dr. Harrison the language is sufficiently Pauline; only 18 words not found elsewhere in Paul are used, and of these three may be disregarded because they are required here for particular purposes which do not arise elsewhere (*cloak, notebooks, copper-smith*).

(2) The only reason that could be given for the invention of such passages as these is the desire to add verisimilitude to pseudepigraphical works, and it is doubtful whether such artless —and in some ways pointless—scraps would have been composed for this purpose. They may be compared with 1 Tim. 1:3 f., 19 f.; 2 Tim. 1:5, 15; 2:17 f.; Tit. 1:5. To this list of more artificial products we should perhaps transfer, from Dr. Harrison's list, 2 Tim. 1:16 ff.; 3:10 f.; 4:6 ff., 14 f. There remains, however, a quantity of material which could have been composed in imitation of genuine Pauline material, but is perhaps better thought of as itself genuine.

(3) These passages can with reasonable probability be fitted into Paul's career. Not all Dr. Harrison's reconstructions are convincing; but it is a striking fact that chronological and topographical notices which, when treated as integral parts of the Pastorals, raise, as we have seen, considerable problems, may, when detached, be quite simply accommodated within the known circumstances of Paul's life.

(4) Scepticism is awakened by the neat distinction of five separate letters, and the elaborate composition assigned to some, especially the last of them. It is difficult to envisage the process by which such letters were first disintegrated and then recombined. It seems more reasonable to suppose that fragments, whose original disposition cannot now be recovered, came into the hands of the author, and that he put them together in a way

that made reasonable sense, but so that we can now say no more than that certain sentences in his Epistles were not composed but received by him.

3. Setting

(a) *The Heresy Attacked.* Controversy plays a large part in the Pastorals. The rise of false doctrine, and the spread of moral evil, are regarded as a sign that the Church has entered upon the last times (1 Tim. 4:1; 2 Tim. 3:1). False teachers, though a check will be set against their activities (2 Tim. 3:9), may be expected to become more numerous, and more pernicious (2 Tim. 3:13). It will be especially necessary for Timothy and Titus, and thus for all ministers and teachers, to be on their guard, to check the first movements of error, to guard the good deposit of faith, and to preserve the sound and trustworthy words of doctrine.

If we ask what was the false doctrine the author had in mind, it is not easy to give a precise answer. He was more concerned to combat the evil moral effect of his adversaries' teaching, and to show up their own moral deficiencies, than to analyse their beliefs. No doubt he was wise; but the result of his staunch refusal to enter into disputation is that our picture of the heretics he reprobated is somewhat cloudy. It may be that they did not all hold precisely the same beliefs, but since we lack the means to discriminate between different groups our best course will be to note the different tendencies which are attacked in various parts of the Pastorals.

(1) The heresy attacked undoubtedly contained a Jewish element; see 1 Tim. 1:7; Tit. 1:10, 14; 3:9 (and on each of these passages see the notes). The law was misused, and there were some who gave heed to Jewish myths—an adjective which may interpret the word 'myth' in other places in which it occurs (1 Tim. 1:4; 4:7; 2 Tim. 4:4). It is not satisfactory to say that these references to error of a Jewish kind arose only out of an attempt by the author to make his work seem Pauline: Paul was known to have disputed with Jews and Judaizers, and these must therefore be brought into the Pauline pseudepigrapha. Nothing in the genuine Pauline letters would suggest an attack on Jewish myths.

(2) The heresy had also a gnostic element. This appears most clearly in 1 Tim. 6:20: 'Keep safe that which has been entrusted to you. Turn a deaf ear to empty and worldly chatter, and the contradictions of so-called "knowledge" (γνῶσις).' It is unlikely (see the notes) that there is a reference here to Marcion and his work *Contradictions*; but it is almost certain that Timothy is being warned against some kind of specious *gnosis*. We may note also the references to genealogies (1 Tim. 1:4; Tit. 3:9), and to myths (1 Tim. 1:4; 4:7; 2 Tim. 4:4; Tit. 1:14); and the false doctrine that the resurrection had already taken place (2 Tim. 2:18). This can only mean a false spiritualizing of the Christian hope, probably due to belief in the essential evil of matter.

(3) The heresy, like all heresies touched with gnosticism, was capable of producing two distinct ways of life. On the one hand, it led to ascetic rigour. The heretics forbade marriage (1 Tim. 4:3; we should compare the positive stress laid on the value of marriage in the Pastorals—1 Tim. 2:15; 5:14; Tit. 2:4), and enjoined abstinence from foods (1 Tim. 4:3; cp. 5:23; Tit. 1:15). Here the natural outcome of gnostic dualism was reinforced by Jewish legalism (cp. 1 Tim. 1:8 f.). On the other hand, the heretics are accused of immoral behaviour (1 Tim. 6:3 ff.; 2 Tim. 3:1–7; Tit. 3:9 ff.).

Our knowledge of the movements of Christian thought in the relevant period is too meagre to enable us to place this heresy (or complex of heresies) precisely. The context, however, in which it may be set is given by the first two observations made above: the context is Jewish gnosticism. It is true that there are some who would regard this term as self-contradictory: what is Jewish cannot be gnostic; what is gnostic cannot be Jewish. The term itself is not worth disputing over. The fact is that a line can be traced from some pre-Christian groups of Jews to Jewish Christian heretics in the second century. The evidence can only be hinted at here. Among the most important links in the chain may be mentioned the Qumran sectaries, who were interested in the knowledge of God, and both taught and practised a modified dualism, closely related with the Old Testament and the observance of the Law. The Essenes described by Josephus were in touch with the beliefs and practices of oriental religions; they lived ascetic lives, rejecting marriage (though a few did not do this), and living on scanty diet. At the other end of the thread

stand the Jewish Christians. Two passages in Ignatius (died
c. A.D. 112) reflect a situation similar to that of the Pastorals.

If any one expound Judaism to you, do not listen to him. For it is
better to listen to Christianity from a circumcised man, than to
Judaism from an uncircumcised man (*Philad.* vi. 1).

Do not be deceived by false opinions, nor by ancient myths
(μυθεύμασιν), which are unprofitable. For if up to now we live
according to the Law in Judaism, we confess that we have not received
grace (*Magnes.* viii. 1).

Plainer evidence is to be found in the Clementine literature. Of
the Jewishness of the Jewish Christianity here attested there can
be no question. See for example *Clementine Recognitions*, i. 43:

They [the priests] often sent to us [Peter and his colleagues], and
asked us to discourse to them concerning Jesus, whether he were the
Prophet whom Moses foretold, who is the eternal Christ. For on this
point only does there seem to be any difference between us who believe in Jesus, and the unbelieving Jews.

Equally clear is the gnosticism of this brand of Christianity.
'Redemption by knowledge is also the subject of the Preachings
of Peter. Jesus as the true prophet must enter the world which is
like a house filled with smoke. He must come from the outside to
open the house, in order that the "light of the sun" may be able
to penetrate there and chase away the "smoke of fire". "The man
who can bring help," says Peter, "I call the true prophet, who
alone can illuminate human souls in such a way that we can dis-
cern with our own eyes the way that leads to eternal salvation."
We find revealed here in its purest form the principle of all
gnosticism. The list of pairs which precede the coming of Adam
set over against each other heaven and earth, sun and moon,
light and fire, day and night, health and sickness, *gnosis* and
ignorance, life and death. It can be seen how, by the gnostic
Leitmotiv, this list is attached to the story of the descent upon
earth of the prophet. The smoke of *fire* which is found inside is
chased away by the *light* of the *sun*, and the result is the redemption of man—life' (O. Cullmann, *Le Problème littéraire et
historique du Roman Pseudo-Clémentin* (1930), pp. 191 f.).

The evidence which has now been sketched would itself be
sufficient to suggest, as their own characteristics make probable, that the background out of which the heretics attacked in
the Pastorals emerged was at the same time Jewish and gnostic,

and that such a background truly existed. It remains to add only one point, the significance of which will shortly appear. Jewish Christianity was strongly anti-Pauline. Paul (often under the guise of Simon Magus) is frequently attacked. One quotation (*Clementine Homilies*, ii. 17) must suffice. Peter declares that, on the basis of the law of pairs (see above), it would be possible

to know on what side Simon, who went before me to the heathen, should be placed, and on what side I myself must be placed, who followed him, as light the darkness, as *gnosis* ignorance, as a cure the disease; thus it is necessary, as the true prophet has told us, that there should come first a false Gospel preached by an impostor, and then the true Gospel. . . .

(b) *Paul and the Gnostics*. Paul then was bitterly attacked by those Jewish gnostic Christians whose heretical kind of Christianity lurks in the background of the Pastorals. He was not friendless in the second century, but some of his friends were no less embarrassing than his enemies. A late New Testament book says of his epistles that

they contain some obscure passages, which the ignorant and unstable misinterpret to their own ruin, as they do the other scriptures (2 Peter 3:16).

These 'ignorant and unstable' persons probably regarded themselves as advanced theologians who were not misinterpreting but rightly expounding Paul's meaning, and claimed him as the authority for their own opinions. The so-called *Gospel of Truth*, an early gnostic production possibly from the pen of Valentinus, contains numerous references to Pauline letters, and Valentinus is said to have been a hearer of one Theodas, himself a companion of Paul's. Indeed, the Valentinians claimed that, for any one who could read, the basic principles of their system were already written in Paul's epistles. Zahn (*Geschichte des neutestamentlichen Kanons*, i (1889), 758) wrote: 'Without the epistles of Paul, Valentinus's doctrine is as unthinkable as without the Prologue of the Fourth Gospel; and it is not by chance that Paul was preferred, by all the Valentinians, as the plainest-spoken preacher of the hidden wisdom.' Again, the Muratorian Canon bears witness to the existence of epistles to the Laodiceans and to the Alexandrians *Pauli nomine finctae ad haeresim Marcionis*. These were probably heretical documents claiming the authority of Paul.

It is a widely recognized fact that (whatever its origin may have been) the Fourth Gospel speedily came into heretical circles, and had to be won back out of the hands of heretics into orthodox Christian use. It seems probable that a somewhat similar fate overtook Paul, though not to anything like the same extent. The great figure of Paul remained high in the admiration of anti-gnostic writers such as Clement, Ignatius, and Polycarp; he was now so firmly seated among the apostles that even the fact that the heretic Marcion could represent himself as the disciple of Paul did not lead to the disowning of the Pauline epistles. Nevertheless, the popularity of Paul with heretics must have led to a good deal of embarrassment.

(c) *Paul and Paulinism Vindicated*. The circumstances that have now been sketched provide a background against which the emergence of the Pastorals can be understood. On the one hand, Paul was attacked by Jewish Christians; on the other, he was accepted and adopted by those whose misapprehension of central Christian truths was imperilling the existence of the Church. Orthodox supporters of Paul had therefore to tread a difficult and narrow path; and it is not unreasonable to see in the Pastorals an attempt to deliver the apostle at the same time from his professed enemies and his false friends. This conclusion may be supported in several ways.

(1) Those who believe ancient works to be pseudonymous should always accept the obligation of explaining why they were published under the name of the reputed author. It is never sufficient to say. 'Such-and-such a work cannot have been written by X, to whom it is ascribed'; it is necessary to give a reason why the work in question should have been published under the name of X. If the suggestion made here is accepted, it is possible to give a much better account of the ascription of the Pastorals to Paul than on any other view. There is no question of the production of historical fiction (as in some of the New Testament apocrypha); nor need we think of a Paulinist who fathered his own writings on the apostle because he admired him so greatly, or of one who happened to have in his possession a few personal jottings from the apostle's pen, and worked them up into three separate letters (one containing none of them!) simply because he could think of no other way of publishing them. The purpose of the Pastorals was practical. Paul was assailed: to Jewish Christians he was 'the enemy', and to many

Gentile Christians he was suspect, or was in danger of becoming suspect, because he was in favour with the gnostics. Those who held fast to the doctrine they had received from their master were under some necessity to publish, to represent in their own generation the genuine Pauline voice. Paul's case should not go by default; being dead, he could yet speak through the pens of those who owed to him their understanding of divine grace.

(2) In the suggested context we can understand with increased clarity and force the personal references to Paul, especially the modest but vehement defence of his rank as an apostle (based as it appears to be on the wording of the genuine letters). Thus 1 Tim. 1:12–16 argues that Paul's appointment is a singular monument of divine grace, which is only magnified (not, as some might argue, nullified) by his previous career as a persecutor. Cp. 2:7; 2 Tim. 1:11; also the reference in 2 Tim. 3:11 to Paul's persecutions, with its sober, almost bitter, comment: Anyone who means to live a godly life as a Christian can expect to be unpopular. In the same way, references to Paul's loneliness gain new force (2 Tim. 1:15; 4:16), and one feels more keenly the description of the aged Paul whose life is poured out as a libation on behalf of an ungrateful Church (2 Tim. 4:6). At the same time, urgent appeals to guard the παραθήκη, or deposit, of sound teaching come into focus (2 Tim. 1:12, 14; and especially 1 Tim. 6:20 f.).

(3) The circumstances we have suggested for the writing of the Pastorals account for the fact that, along with emphasis on the authentic Pauline Gospel, there go certain over-emphases, which have the effect of suggesting that Paul was rather a safe, middle-of-the-road man, than the uncompromising fighter we know him to have been. It was necessary for the Pauline 'figure' reconstructed some decades after the apostle's death to walk carefully along the middle of the road, and to steer clear of Judaism and gnosticism alike; not only to steer clear of them— the historical Paul could do that—but manifestly to steer clear of them. The result is often pedestrian; but it is intelligible, and it was of the highest possible value, for it projected the work and influence of Paul into a new generation, and retained for him his place as *Doctor Gentium*, the teacher of the Gentile Church in one of the most significant and dangerous periods in its history. In this period the Pastorals represented him with incomplete, but sufficient accuracy; and they did more, for it is to some extent

due to the Pastorals that, notwithstanding frontal attack and misunderstanding, the greater epistles of the real Paul held their place in the Canon.

(d) *Date and Place of Writing.* It is not possible to name the author of the Pastorals. It seems evident (though it has been disputed) that he wrote before Polycarp wrote his epistle (or epistles); this means that we cannot date the Pastorals later than A.D. 125. The argument that they were written against Marcion (which would upset this conclusion) remains unconvincing. No *terminus ad quem* earlier than A.D. 125 can be fixed by external evidence. 2 Tim. 3:11, if, as is probable, it reflects knowledge of Acts, provides a *terminus post quem*, but a very unsatisfactory one, for to say that the Pastorals were written later than Acts is helpful (as far as dating is concerned) only if the date of Acts is known, and this is in fact far from certain. It is, however, unlikely that Acts was written before the 80's or 90's, and accordingly we may, with considerable hesitation, place the Pastorals in the period A.D. 90–125.

This interval can be narrowed only by means of arguments which are necessarily subjective. Of these the following three may be mentioned, though, as will appear, they can be used only with reserve.

(1) It has been observed that there is a good deal of similarity in general style and theme between the Pastorals and 1 Clement (*c.* A.D. 96), and that the epistles of Ignatius (*c.* A.D. 112), to a more limited extent, bear witness to similar circumstances. These considerations might suggest a date near to both these documents, but nearer to the former—perhaps A.D. 100. This may well be true; but doubt is awakened by the fact that Polycarp recalls the Pastorals more clearly than does Ignatius. This does not prove that the Pastorals were written in Polycarp's time rather than Ignatius's, but it throws into question the method of argument employed.

(2) Arguments are sometimes based upon the kind of gnostic error combated in the Epistles. This (it is sometimes said) is undeveloped, and those who maintain it are still tolerated, and disciplined, as members of the Church; the Epistles must therefore be fairly early (that is, not much later than A.D. 100). This may be true; but the argument can be advanced with confidence only by those who find it possible to trace and date the development of 'Christian Gnosticism' from the so-called Colossian

heresy to the work of Valentinus in the middle of the second century.

(3) Similar criticism may be applied to arguments based on the development of the Christian ministry. If the ministry had everywhere developed in the same way and at the same rate, and if the story of its development were fully known to us, we should be able to date the Pastorals by considering what they tell us about ministers. Neither of the necessary conditions is satisfied. It is, however, true and significant that the Pastorals show none of the elaborate development of the ministry that would require us to date them late in the second century.

One further point calls for notice. Much of what has been said above about the setting of the Epistles could be said, *mutatis mutandis*, about Acts, and it may well be that Acts and the Pastorals were not widely separate in time and place of origin.

It is often thought that 2 Timothy, which appears to contain the largest number of genuine Pauline fragments, was the earliest of our epistles, and that 1 Timothy, which may be said to reflect the most developed ecclesiastical situation, was the latest. This too may be true; but it is quite uncertain, and does not greatly illuminate the Epistles, which can be read independently.

There is practically no evidence to inform us where the Pastorals were written. In view of references in the Epistles themselves to Ephesus and the province of Asia (1 Tim. 1:3; 2 Tim. 1:15, 18; 4:12), and of the quotations in Polycarp (bishop of Smyrna), there is perhaps no better guess than that they were written in this neighbourhood—a notable centre of early Christian literature, and possibly the place where the Pauline letters were collected. But it would be a serious mistake to regard this as more than a plausible guess.

Far more important than these conjectures is the theological content of the Pastorals.

4. *Theology and Practice*

(a) *Man and Sin*. Man was created by God (1 Tim. 2:13, assuming the narrative of Genesis), who made him for himself (1 Tim. 2:4). The whole of God's creation was in itself good (1 Tim. 4:4), since God made it, and inanimate creation remains good; but man has fallen from the condition in which he was created. The woman, Eve, was deceived, and fell into sin (1 Tim. 2:14). It is not stated here but it is certainly implied that the male creature also fell into sin, since it is assumed that the race as a whole is sinful; but from Eve's priority in sin women have inherited a subordinate position, so that in marriage the husband must necessarily take the predominant place, and must not be governed by his wife. It is clear from the Epistles as a whole both that women are equally with men the objects of God's love and salvation, and that they are expected to express their response to God in a different way.

The connexion between the seduction of Eve and the present state of mankind is not made clear in our Epistles; but it is evident that they regard all men as sinful and therefore in need of salvation (1 Tim. 1:15; 2:4; 5:24 f.; 6:16; 2 Tim. 3:13; 4:3; Tit. 1:11 f.; 3:3). There is no definition of sin, but several passages describe in some detail the ways in which it is expressed: words used are jealousy, quarrelling, slander, base suspicions, endless wrangles (1 Tim. 6:4); empty and worldly chatter (2 Tim. 2:16); love of money and self, arrogance, boastfulness, abusiveness, ingratitude, impiety, implacable hatred, intemperate ferocity, treachery, self-importance, lack of filial respect (2 Tim. 3:2 f.); slavery to passion and pleasure, malice, envy (Tit. 3:3). Sins such as these are self-evident; there are others, however, which are no less sinful because they are less apparent (1 Tim. 5:24).

Sin is expected to grow more grievous in the last times, to which the Epistles refer. In this it goes hand in hand with heresy, and the close connexion between the two is not accidental: wrong belief engenders wrong action. This development of error has been prophesied: 'The Spirit says expressly that in after times some will desert from the faith and give their minds to subversive doctrines inspired by devils, through the specious falsehoods of men whose own conscience is branded with the devil's sign' (1 Tim. 4:1 f.; cp. 2 Tim. 2:16 f.). From teaching which neglects the wholesome precepts of Jesus Christ come jealousy, quarrelling, slander, and the like (1 Tim. 6:3 f.). The final age of this world is to be a time of troubles. Men will love nothing but money and self (2 Tim. 3:1 f.).

Notwithstanding its increasing wickedness, God continues to be concerned for the well-being of the whole human race (though 1 Tim. 4:10 adds, 'above all, of believers'). He sent his Son as the Saviour of sinners (1 Tim. 1. 15), and desires that all men should be saved (1 Tim. 2. 4). This 'all' includes even the most unlikely: Paul himself, the persecutor (1 Tim. 1:13–16); rulers (1 Tim. 2:2); the troublesome Jews; and the Cretans, who are of outstanding wickedness (Tit. 1:10–14).

Man's life, under God's providence, is a time of training and discipline. We brought nothing into the world, and we can take nothing out (1 Tim. 6:7). Between our naked entry into the world and our naked departure from it, we must not love this age (2 Tim. 4:10), but live with our attention focused upon God's future (see below); the resurrection has not yet taken place (2 Tim. 2:18), and this world must not be valued too highly. The athlete preparing for a race practises training of the body (1 Tim. 4:8); the Christian must be equally diligent in the practice of religious training (e.g. 2 Tim. 2:25; 3:16; Tit. 2:12). The rich, for example, must not fix their hopes on so uncertain a thing as money (1 Tim. 6:17). Insistence on a disciplined life must not, however, be confused with asceticism of a dualistic kind, against which the Pastorals contend vehemently. It is wrong to urge abstinence from foods and from marriage (1 Tim. 4:3 f.); God himself endows us richly with all things to enjoy (1 Tim. 6:17). In this world, a man should work for his living, and in order to have the means of helping others (Tit. 3:8, 14); Timothy must cease to abstain from wine (1 Tim. 5:23). To the pure all things are pure (Tit. 1:15).

(b) *Salvation: Eschatology.* All men, having as sinners lost the state of blessedness for which they were created, are in need of salvation; and it is the will of God that all should be saved. This is stated explicitly in 1 Tim. 2:4, and implied by other passages, such as 1 Tim. 1:15: if the salvation effected by Christ was such as to embrace even the first (that is, the chief) of sinners it follows that none is excluded from its scope. God is the Saviour of all men (1 Tim. 4:10).

Salvation was effected by the sending into the world of Jesus Christ; our Epistles describe both God the Father (1 Tim. 1:1; 2:3; 4:10; Tit. 1:3; 2:10; 3:4) and Jesus Christ (2 Tim. 1:10; Tit. 1:4; 3:6) by the word Saviour, and this reflects the conviction that the ultimate design of salvation arises from the depths of the divine mind, and was executed through the life and death of the Son. The theme of the Christian Gospel may be described as 'the glory of God in his eternal felicity' (1 Tim. 1:11), and equally as 'Jesus Christ, risen from the dead, born of David's line' (2 Tim. 2:8). The work of salvation rests upon God's mercy and grace alone, and in no way upon the desert or achievement of man. '[God] brought us salvation . . . not for any merit of ours but of his own purpose and his own grace' (2 Tim. 1:9); in Christ, 'the grace of God has dawned upon the world' (Tit. 2:11), and the 'kindness and generosity of God our Saviour dawned upon the world, . . . not for any good deeds of our own, but because he was merciful . . . [we were] justified by his grace' (Tit. 3: 4–7).

The work of Christ had the effect of salvation because of his own mediating position between God and man (1 Tim. 2:5 f.; see also below), and because in his death he 'sacrificed himself to win freedom for all mankind' (1 Tim. 2:6; cp. Tit. 2:14). How the death of Jesus came to be a sacrificial ransom-price ($\dot{a}\nu\tau\dot{\iota}\lambda\nu$-$\tau\rho\rho\nu$) is never explained in the Pastoral Epistles. The death of Jesus was followed by his resurrection (2 Tim. 2:8, 11; cp. 1 Tim. 3:16), and his triumph over the power of sin and death brought life and immortality to light (2 Tim. 1:10).

Salvation, though potentially universal in its scope, is in fact limited in its extent. God who is the Saviour of all men is the Saviour especially of believers (1 Tim. 4:10). It is a mark of the days in which the Pastorals were written, the 'last days' as the author believed them to be, that though some embraced the salvation offered them through the Gospel others plunged deeper and deeper into wickedness and error (see above, p. 20). Whether the author regarded such men as beyond hope it is difficult to say; Hymenaeus and Philetus had been consigned to Satan 'in the hope that through this discipline they might learn not to be blasphemous' (1 Tim. 1:20). This may mean that they were to be restored by some kind of disciplinary process; but they were in any case perverted members of the Church, not unbelievers. It is by faith that salvation in Jesus Christ is received. Paul the persecutor was chosen as an outstanding example of 'all who were in future to *have faith* in him and gain eternal life' (1 Tim. 1:16). Christians may be described as 'those who have come to believe in God' (Tit. 3:8). Faith ($\pi\dot{\iota}\sigma\tau\iota\varsigma$), then, is the means by which men lay hold upon Jesus Christ, and the salvation which he gives (e.g. 2 Tim. 3:15). As such, it is essentially a personal relation. This appears when, in Paul's name, the author declares, 'I know the one whom I have trusted ($\pi\epsilon\pi\dot{\iota}\sigma\tau\epsilon\nu\kappa\alpha$), and am confident of his power to keep safe what he has put into my charge' (2 Tim. 1:12). The same word is also used in a less personal sense, as when 'the faith' stands for Christianity (e.g. 1 Tim. 3:9), and men are urged to keep (the) faith, that is, to show faithfulness (e.g. 2 Tim. 4:7). The author thus differs to some extent from Paul himself, though like Paul he too knows well that Christianity is more than a steady but superficial adherence to 'the faith', and attacks those who 'preserve the outward form of religion, but are a standing denial of its reality' (2 Tim. 3:5).

The Pastorals expressly repudiate (see above, pp. 21 f.) the notion that human works can contribute to the process of salvation, which is the fruit of God's grace only; there are, however, passages (which may be compared with those just noted) where the author comes near to contradicting himself: see especially 1 Tim. 1:13 (where Paul is 'dealt with mercifully' 'because [he] acted ignorantly in unbelief'); also perhaps 1 Tim. 2:15 (with the note), and 2 Tim. 2:19 ff. It is probably only just to say that in what might appear his Pelagian passages the author has been impelled by excess of zeal for the moral consequences of faith to overstress the ethical element in Christian life.

It should be noted that in Tit. 3:5 the place of baptism in salvation is mentioned. In the context stands a denial of the validity of good deeds of our own, and an insistence upon justification by grace.

Paul himself commonly speaks of salvation as a future event; that is, he uses the term to denote not an inward and present experience of the Christian in this age but the final act by which God consummates his purpose for mankind. In the Pastorals, salvation is sometimes an event that has happened, and a present possession (e.g. 1 Tim. 4:16; Tit. 3:5). A future outlook is nevertheless also maintained. For the future activity of Jesus Christ as Judge and Saviour see below; towards this the author constantly looks for the fulfilment of the work which is already begun. The Spirit has been bestowed so that 'we might in hope become heirs to eternal life' (Tit. 3:7). Naturally, Christians look forward with longing to receiving this inheritance. They have set their hearts on Christ's coming (2 Tim. 4:8), and Paul, confident of the prize, is sure that the Lord will keep him 'safe until his heavenly reign begins' (2 Tim. 4:18). Similarly (1 Tim. 6:14), Timothy is charged 'to obey your orders irreproachably and without fault until our Lord Jesus

Christ appears'. Like other New Testament writers, the author of the Pastorals believes this future salvation to be partially realized in the present. Eternal life is something which Christians may hope to inherit in the future (Tit. 3:7, quoted above; also 1:2; 2 Tim. 1:1), but they may grasp it now (1 Tim. 6:12, 19; cp. 4:8). In many parts of the New Testament the Holy Spirit is thought of as the means by which the future is brought into the present, and this thought is not absent from the Pastorals (1 Tim. 3:16; 2 Tim. 1:7, 14; Tit. 3:5), and though the Spirit is very infrequently mentioned in the Pastorals (so infrequently that many have found here a strong argument against Pauline authorship), it is fair to say of the Pastorals that 'The paradox of Christian existence—a new existence within this old world (Tit. 2:12)—is here grasped: in other words the qualitative (and not merely chronological) sense of the Christian's "betweenness" is grasped' (R. Bultmann, *Theology of the New Testament*, ii (1955), 185).

(c) *Jesus Christ.* Jesus Christ was a man; this is stated emphatically, but only once (1 Tim. 2:5; cp. also 1 Tim. 6:13; 2 Tim. 2:8). Other terms, which bring out the supernatural and divine aspects of his person, are frequent. Most common is the term Lord (κύριος), which is used at 1 Tim. 1:2, 12, (14); 6:3, 14; 2 Tim. 1:8, 16, 18; 2:7, (19), 24 f.; 3:11; 4:8, 14, 22. In some of these passages it is not certain whether the word applies to Jesus Christ or to God the Father; in several of them it may be a more or less conventional title, but 1 Tim. 6:15 shows that the author of the Pastorals took the divine lordship very seriously. In this verse (on which see the note) the reference is probably not to Jesus Christ, but we may justly infer from it that in other passages too the words Lord and King carry great weight.

As the Lord, the holder of supreme authority over the whole human race, Jesus Christ exercises the two functions of Judge and Saviour. For the former, see 2 Tim. 1:18; 4:1, 8; cp. 1 Tim. 6:13 f. All, whether they die before the *parousia* or not, must give an account of themselves to Christ. Jesus Christ is described as 'the Saviour' at Tit. 1:4; 3:6, and there are several passages (1 Tim. 2:3; 4:10; Tit. 1:3; 2:10, 13; 3:4) which refer to 'God our Saviour', without making it clear whether the reference is to the first or second Person of the Trinity. It seems natural to refer most of them to the Father, and there is no difficulty in the description of both the Father and the Son by the same term (cp. p. 24); but at Tit. 2:13 it seems probable (though not quite certain) that we should render, '. . . . our great God and Saviour Christ Jesus'.

Jesus Christ, then, is both man and God—the latter term is no more than the result of taking seriously his office as Judge and Saviour, and his status as Lord. He is thus able to be the Mediator, the one Mediator, between God and men (1 Tim. 2:5; see the note). By 'Mediator' the Pastorals do not mean a *tertium quid*, half God and half man, but one who truly was man, and by his obedient and sacrificial life and death as man reconciled God and his creatures. He was not a Prometheus, not an angel, not a gnostic revealer, not a divine man; but man *and* God, the man in whom the divisive effect of sin was removed so that deity and humanity might be one.

Christum cognoscere, beneficia eius cognoscere: Christ is Mediator, reconciler, in virtue of what he has done; and the great saving events as noted in the Pastorals must now be recalled. There is a possible, but perhaps unlikely, reference to the birth of Christ in 1 Tim. 2:15 (see the note), but before this event he existed in relation to God and to the work of salvation. This is implied by the statement that he *came* into the world (1 Tim. 1:15), and was manifested (1 Tim. 3:16), and also by the statement that grace was 'granted to us in Christ Jesus from all eternity' (2 Tim. 1:9). Of the earthly life of Jesus no more is said until we come to his trial before Pilate (1 Tim. 6:13) and his death (1 Tim. 2:6; (2 Tim. 2:11); Tit. 2:14). He was raised from the dead (1 Tim. 3:16; 2 Tim. 1:10; 2:8), and glorified (1 Tim. 3:16; 2 Tim. 2:12). The fewness of these references to the death and exaltation of Christ, in comparison with those in the genuine Pauline letters, will be immediately apparent. Jesus Christ now reigns in glory, but will on the great Day come again, and take those who faithfully wait for him to share in his glory (1 Tim. (1:2); 6:14 f.; 2 Tim. 1:12, 18; 2:12, 18; 4:1, 8, 14, 18). The fact that he is thus the central figure at every stage in the work of salvation underlines the assertion noted earlier that he is the one Mediator between God and men.

(*d*) *Ethics*. The assertion that the Pastorals contain a moralized version of Paulinism is not without foundation. Paul himself was deeply concerned for the moral behaviour of his churches, but he always makes clear the theological and Christocentric basis of the moral demands that he makes. It cannot be said that the

Pastorals always do this. Lists of moral duties are laid down, and sometimes at least appear to exist in their own right, and as ends complete in themselves. To recognize this, however, is not

Christian marriage, depicted in a fourth-century medallion (Rome). For the ideal of marriage in the Pastorals see, for example, 1 Tim. 4:3; 5:14; Tit. 2:4 f.

to deny that truly Christian motives do underlie the ethical teaching of the Pastorals, though it must be admitted that these are sometimes far from evident.

It is God himself who commands the good life: this is its sufficient ground. 'The aim and object' contemplated by God's command 'is the love which springs from a clean heart, from a good conscience, and from faith that is genuine' (1 Tim. 1:5). The life which God commands he will also reward. At the end of his course, Paul can say, 'And now the prize awaits me, the garland of righteousness which the Lord, the all-just Judge, will award me on that great Day' (2 Tim. 4:8). By his obedient life, Paul has set an example which Christians should follow (2 Tim. 3:10 f.), and Timothy and Titus in turn must set an example (1 Tim. 4:12; Tit. 2:7). Christian ethics may be said to have a natural ground in the fact that 'we brought nothing into the world, because when we leave it we cannot take anything with us either' (1 Tim. 6:7). It follows from this that men should be cheerfully content with the necessaries of life, and avoid all the perils and evils that arise from the love of money (1 Tim. 6:10). This emphasis upon quiet contentment (cp. 1 Tim. 2:2) with a simple life is not to be confounded with ethical dualism, which, in itself and in its consequences, the Pastorals regard as essentially evil. It is wrong to forbid marriage (1 Tim. 4:3), and to enjoin abstinence from foods and wine (1 Tim. 4:3; 5:23; 6:17). God has given men all things richly to enjoy, and if Timothy is urged to accept the hard lot of a Christian this is as far removed as can be from asceticism. He is called to the life of a Christian soldier (1 Tim. 1:18; 2 Tim. 2:3), not that of an anchorite. Christians must behave well for the sake of the Church's reputation (1 Tim. 3:7; 6:1; Tit. 2:5; 3:8, 14); yet Christian ethics are not an economy, but a natural product of the Christian religious life (1 Tim. 1:5, 19; 2:2; 5:4, 10; 2 Tim. 1:16 f.; 2:19; Tit. 1:15; 2:11 f.; &c.). It is here that we may see implied the great Pauline fundamentals of death with Christ to sin, and the life of gratitude and love; but it must be admitted that in the Pastorals these are scarcely more than implications.

The virtues actually enjoined upon the readers of the Epistles are in large part the civic virtues widely acknowledged (if by no means universally practised) in the Hellenistic world; see notes on 1 Tim. 3:1–7; Tit. 2:4. These are the virtues that make the world go round: the honesty of a good conscience; self-discipline; a record generally free from blame and the possibility of reproach. They are, however, leavened with virtues more specifically Christian, as when love stands alongside self-discipline in 2 Tim. 1:7. It is characteristic of the Pastorals that these virtues are specifically applied to different groups in the community, marked out by age, sex, or social status. The

Epistles are particularly concerned with the moral qualities of Church officers and enrolled widows; see 1 Tim. 3:1–16; 5:10; Tit. 1:5–9. It is, however, noteworthy that, though it is evident that leading officials are singled out because of their responsibilities, their opportunity for setting an example, and the danger which a lapse on their part could cause, the virtues required in them are the same as those sought in Christians generally. All are expected to respond to the Gospel in a life of appropriate moral effort.

(e) *Worship.* It is the Church that meets to offer worship to God; for consideration of the Church itself see the next section. We are concerned here with the various elements of which its worship is composed. These appear very clearly in the Pastorals.

It is of primary importance (1 Tim. 2:1: 'First of all') that *prayer* should be offered, on behalf of all mankind. It is the men of the community (all of them, apparently) who pray aloud, raising their hands toward heaven, whereas the women take part in modest silence (1 Tim. 2:8 f.); though the latter, especially widows, have their own part to play (1 Tim. 3:11; 5:5; see also pp. 29, 32).

It is probable that hymns were sung, and that fragments of some of these are quoted at 1 Tim. 3:16; 2 Tim. 2:11 ff. (see the notes). If it is said that these are as much like creeds as hymns, it may be replied that this is true of many of the greatest hymns. Other 'faithful sayings', however, may be classed as rudimentary summaries of Christian belief, perhaps used as such in worship. These are: 1 Tim. 1:15; 4:9 f.; Tit. 3:6 ff. From these passages it would be possible to construct a statement as follows:

It is to be believed that
    (1) God is the Saviour of all men.
    (2) Christ Jesus came into the world to save sinners.
    (3) He died and rose from the dead.
    (4) The Holy Spirit has been poured forth.
    (5) Baptism is for regeneration.
    (6) We may hope for eternal life.

But it must be acknowledged that the material has to be forced into this conventional mould.

Another element in public worship is the reading of scripture: 1 Tim. 4:13; cp. 2 Tim. 3:15 f. Evidently of great importance is the sermon. The recipients of the letters are repeatedly enjoined to preach the word without intermission (1 Tim. 4:11, 13, 15 f.; 6:2, 17; 2 Tim. 2:2, 14 f., 25; 4:1 f., 5; Tit. 2:1, 7, 15). Some of these passages undoubtedly refer to the work of evangelism rather than to the worship of Christians, and some to private instruction and admonition; but there can equally be no doubt of the place of preaching and teaching (λόγος and διδασκαλία) in the life of the Church. In this Timothy and Titus are joined by elders (1 Tim. 5:17), and we may compare also the references to prophecy (1 Tim. 1:18; 4:14).

Of the sacraments, baptism is plainly referred to at Tit. 3:5; there is no reference or even allusion to the eucharist.

In addition we should note here that Church meetings, including probably meetings for worship, were presided over by elders (1 Tim. 5:17), and that bishops and deacons took their place in the work of teaching and controversy; see further below for their work and appointment. Teaching by women was forbidden, or rather strictly limited; for with 1 Tim. 2:12 compare 5:5, 10 and Tit. 2:4.

(f) *The Church and the Ministry*. At least since the time of the Muratorian Canon, where it is noted that, though personal letters, they were valued *in ordinationem ecclesiasticae disciplinae*, the Pastorals have been recognized as dealing more directly than any other part of the New Testament with the Church as an organization. The work and status of Timothy and Titus themselves, and of other ministers referred to in the Epistles under various titles, have been discussed at great length, and often with controversial intent. The basic facts may be set out as follows:

(1) Independently of any question with regard to its visible constitution, the Church evidently occupies an important place in the work of salvation. It is the 'pillar and bulwark of the truth' (1 Tim. 3:15). This does not mean that the truth (that is, the Gospel) is dependent upon the Church, and would fail without it, but that the Church exists to serve the truth. What the Church is, is plainly declared in the 'firm foundation' (2 Tim. 2:19), which bears 'this inscription: "The Lord knows his own", and, "Everyone who takes the Lord's name upon his lips must forsake wickedness" '. Compare 2 Tim. 2:10 ('God's chosen ones'). The Church is the elect community created and called forth by God's gracious election in Jesus Christ, and

commissioned to act in the interests of the Gospel which declares this truth.

(2) The second part of 2 Tim. 2:19 leads to a further point. Since every member of the Church thus constituted by the Gospel is under obligation to forsake evil it is necessary for the Church to exercise discipline. This obligation is sharpened by the fact that in the 'last times', in which the Church lives, both false doctrine and bad living may be expected to become prevalent (1 Tim. 4:1 ff.; 2 Tim. 3:1–5; 4:3 f.). Against false doctrine, the Church must maintain the truth, and, if possible, convict heretics of their error. At the same time, it must build up its members in faith and love, in order that obedient Christian life may be lived; and those who go astray must be rebuked, and, in case of final necessity, excluded from the community.

(3) On this basis the teaching of the Pastorals about the ministry can be set forth and understood. It is primarily, though not exclusively, through those who hold office within the Church that the Gospel is proclaimed, taught, and defended, and Christian discipline administered. It is for this purpose that ministers are called by God, though not all of them fulfil their office in the same way.

(4) The Pastorals look back to Paul as the apostle and minister *par excellence*, though his figure is seen through a haze of hero-worship. His conversion and call gave him a special commission as herald, apostle, and teacher (1 Tim. 1:12 f.; 2:7; 2 Tim. 1:11; Tit. 1:3), and his role in administering discipline in the Church is manifest, both in the general tone of authority which pervades the letters, and in particular instances such as 1 Tim. 1:19 f. This authority is not one that can be observed or estimated by human standards; what is visible in Paul as the outward characteristic of ministry is suffering (2 Tim. 3:10 ff.). The word of God is and must be free, but its preacher is in chains (2 Tim. 2:9).

(5) Timothy and Titus are represented as Paul's assistants. This is doubtless what they were, but it is well to remember that we may not assume that the historical data of these pseudonymous Epistles are necessarily true. This does not greatly affect their teaching on the ministry, but it means that the two assistants are less historical personages in a unique historical setting ('apostolic delegates', perhaps) than types of the ministry in general. Timothy was ordained to his ministry by prophecy with

the laying on of hands (1 Tim. 4:14; 2 Tim. 1:6), and there was thereby given him a spiritual gift (χάρισμα) for the carrying out of his duties. It is evident that this gift was one that could be neglected or lost; that is, that it operated in Timothy's faithful execution of his task.

This task was primarily that of evangelism (see especially 2 Tim. 4:1–5) and preaching (*passim*; see p. 29). Preaching means prophesying (1 Tim. 1:18; 4:14), expounding the Old Testament (2 Tim. 3:16), and teaching (1 Tim. 4:6, 13, 16; 2 Tim. 3:10, 16; Tit. 2:1, 7). All these activities concern the deposit (παραθήκη) of truth which God has entrusted to men in the Gospel (1 Tim. 6:20; 2 Tim. 1:12, 14); the last in particular passes readily over into the work of caring for the faithful as their pastor, and showing them, by example as well as precept, how Christians should live (1 Tim. 4:12; Tit. 2:7). Included in this duty is that of resisting error, and those who propagate it (1 Tim. 1:3; 2 Tim. 2:25; Tit. 1:13; 3:10 f.). Finally, Paul's assistants, who are continuing his work, must themselves have an eye to the future; Timothy must teach faithful men who in turn will teach others (2 Tim. 2:2; it is evident that continuity lies in the *teaching*).

(6) Among these 'faithful men' are no doubt the ministers whom we meet in the Pastorals. Their work, it seems, is primarily within the community rather than directly evangelistic; otherwise, their activities correspond closely with those of Timothy and Titus. They are responsible for maintaining the truth by preaching and teaching, and by resisting adversaries; for presiding over God's household, the Church; for caring for its members, instructing them in Christian living, and setting them a good example (1 Tim. 3:1–16; 5:17–22; 2 Tim. 2:2; Tit. 1:5–9). Some of them at least are paid for their work (1 Tim. 5:17 f.), and it is of the first importance that they should be good Christian men, of good repute both within and without the Church. Thus their activities also, like those of Paul, and of Timothy and Titus, are grounded in the Gospel and the discipline.

It is important to note the names which are given to these ministers, though the terminology is too fluid to allow firm historical conclusions. For example, the word διάκονος ('deacon') is applied to Timothy (1 Tim. 4:6), and the corresponding abstract noun (διακονία) to both Paul and Timothy (1 Tim. 1:12;

2 Tim. 4:5). In a more technical sense, the word *deacon* is used only in 1 Tim. 3:8–13, but this paragraph describes only the requisite qualifications, and not the duties of deacons. We may guess that these included the care of the poor, but this is no more than a guess. *Elders* or *presbyters* (πρεσβύτεροι) are mentioned only in 1 Tim. 5:17 ff. and Tit. 1:5. Clearly they occupy a leading role in the Church; at least some of them 'preside', and some of them preside well. Some but not all 'labour at preaching and teaching'. They resemble the governing body of a synagogue. It is disputed whether the word *bishop* (ἐπίσκοπος) describes the same persons as presbyter (elder), but this seems to be clearly implied by Tit. 1:5 ff. The office of 'leadership' (1 Tim. 3:1; for the qualifications sought in leaders, or bishops, see 3:2–7; Tit. 1:7 ff.) is probably equivalent to that of presiding (1 Tim. 5:17). It is, however, proper to see in this verse signs of that process by which some presbyters came to an eminence beyond that of their fellows.

Among the ministers so far mentioned women have no place. This fact arises not out of prejudice, but from theological grounds (1 Tim. 2:13 f.; see above, pp. 19 f.), and by no means denies to women the possibility of Christian vocation. In addition to the truly Christian vocation to be wives and mothers, they have a specific sphere of service as widows (1 Tim. 5:3–16), and 1 Tim. 3:11 *may* refer to deaconesses. Compare also Tit. 2:4. The root of the matter is that it is contrary to the divine order of creation that women should exercise dominance over men, particularly over their husbands; but it must be remembered that the Pastorals themselves express the truth that ministerial authority (even Paul's) consists not in dominance, but in διακονία (ministry, service).

(*g*) *The Pastorals in the New Testament*. Except for the ecclesiastical controversialist, who sees an opportunity of scoring points about the constitution and practices of the Church in an otherwise obscure period, the Pastorals cannot be said to be one of the more exciting parts of the New Testament; and indeed they contain little enough live ammunition for the controversialist. For the Pastorals do not show us 'Primitive Catholicism' (whether this be taken as a term of praise or of opprobrium), so much as developed Paulinism. The issues which made Paul's own Paulinism live are gone: Judaizers of the old kind no longer threaten the peace, and even the existence, of the Church, and the place of Gentiles is so comfortably assured that the author seems unaware of the theological struggles and revolutions which preceded their admission. Of the growing gnostic peril, which helped to evoke the Johannine literature at the end of the first century, the author is aware, but unlike John he reacts to it only negatively. He has no wish to say anything new; but he is desperately concerned not to lose his grip on what he knows to be old and good, and to hand it on to the new age.

Herein lies the greatest importance of the Pastorals. Not their only importance; for many elements of Christian truth are stated clearly, powerfully, and unforgettably in these letters, so that they have an importance in their own right, in virtue of their positive contribution to the understanding of Jesus Christ and his work, and of Christian obedience. Yet it is true that if we wish to read of justification by faith we shall turn to Romans and Galatians; if we wish to study Christology we shall read Colossians and the Fourth Gospel; if we wish to understand the meaning of sacrifice we shall seek it in Hebrews. The Pastorals are not seminal works, as those are. They represent rather a first attempt to do what each generation of Christians must attempt—to restate the convictions of the first, apostolic generation, in a new era and a new environment. That is to say, the Pastorals instruct us in what is our own task; for it is no concern of ours whether external circumstances and our own gifts combine to kindle the spark of originality and creativity, but it is our duty to 'join the struggle in defence of the faith, the faith which God entrusted to his people once and for all' (Jude 3). If therefore the Pastorals insist upon the primary importance of maintaining in its purity the Gospel message of God's gracious activity—past, present, and future—in Jesus Christ; if they insist upon the necessity of Church discipline, and high standards of Christian obedience; if they require that Christian ministers shall be men of irreproachable character and competent attainment: from these affirmations the Church of every generation may learn its own task.

So far the Pastorals have been treated as Church tracts written at the close of the first century. This historical approach to them is helpful, and in no way wrong; but it must not be forgotten that they confront the reader as part of the New Testament, and thus as one element in the apostolic testimony that God has caused to be borne to his Son. They are accordingly not merely an example that Christians of later generations may or may not follow as they think fit, but part of the scriptural conversation between the Holy Spirit and the Church, in which the Spirit (using on this occasion the voice of an unknown author but speaking with his own divine authority) recalls and applies the things of Christ, and convicts of sin, righteousness, and judgement. Students have too often approached the Pastorals with the (perhaps unconscious) assumption that given the opportunity they could have written the Epistles very much better themselves. It is only a humbler and more reverent approach that will find the sometimes hidden splendour of these letters.

LITERATURE

In addition to general books on introduction to the New Testament, the theology of the New Testament, and the history of the primitive Church, which are too numerous to be mentioned here, the following will be found useful in the study of the Pastoral Epistles:

J. H. BERNARD, *The Pastoral Epistles*. Cambridge Greek Testament, 1922.

J. CALVIN, *Commentaries on the Epistles to Timothy, Titus, and Philemon*, 1st edn. 1556; Calvin Translation Society, 1856.

M. DIBELIUS, *Die Pastoralbriefe*. Handbuch zum Neuen Testament, xiii, 3rd edn. revised by H. Conzelmann, 1955.

B. S. EASTON, *The Pastoral Epistles*, 1948.

R. FALCONER, *The Pastoral Epistles*, 1937.

D. GUTHRIE, *The Pastoral Epistles*. Tyndale New Testament Commentaries, 1957.

P. N. HARRISON, *The Problem of the Pastoral Epistles*, 1921.

J. JEREMIAS, *Die Briefe an Timotheus und Titus*. Das Neue Testament Deutsch, 4th ed., 1947.

W. LOCK, *A Critical and Exegetical Commentary on the Pastoral Epistles*. International Critical Commentary, 1924.

R. ST. J. PARRY, *The Pastoral Epistles*, 1920.

A. SCHLATTER, *Die Kirche der Griechen im Urteil des Paulus*, 1936.

E. F. SCOTT, *The Pastoral Epistles*. The Moffatt New Testament Commentary, 1936.

E. K. SIMPSON, *The Pastoral Epistles*, 1954.

C. SPICQ, *Les Épîtres pastorales*. Études Bibliques, 3rd edn., 1947.

Commentaries have occasionally been cited under the author's name only.

T.W.N.T. means *Theologisches Wörterbuch zum Neuen Testament*, founded by G. Kittel, now edited by G. Friedrich.

ANALYSIS

Titus

1 TIMOTHY

1 FROM Paul, apostle of Christ Jesus by command of God
2 our Saviour and Christ Jesus our hope, to Timothy his true-
born son in the faith.

Grace, mercy, and peace to you from God the Father and
Christ Jesus our Lord.

---

1. 1:1, 2. THE ADDRESS

Without exception, the Pauline letters follow the style of
address common in Greek letter-writing: A to B, greeting. The
names of both sender and recipient, and the greeting, are however qualified in a specifically Christian sense, generally in such
a way as to bring out basic truths of the Christian faith. In the
Pastorals, Paul is described as an *apostle*, though this word is
differently expanded in the three letters; the recipients are his
children (his *true-born son*, 1 Tim. 1:2; Tit. 1:4; his *dear son*,
2 Tim. 1:2); and to the 'grace and peace' found in every genuine
epistle is added in 1 and 2 Timothy *mercy*. Each of these epistolary
prefaces sets the scene which the Pastorals as a whole presuppose.
Paul the aged, an apostle of divine appointment, addresses and
instructs his younger but trusted representatives.

1 *Paul, apostle of Christ Jesus.* For Paul's apostleship in the Pastorals,
see Introduction, p. 30. Here, as at Tit. 1:3 (cp. Gal. 1:1, 12), Paul
emphasizes that his apostleship is not of human origin but springs
from the *command* (a word used of divine oracles) *of God*. He is not a
self-appointed propagandist, but an authorized representative of
God himself. The character of his apostleship is determined by the
nature of the God who sends him: *God our Saviour and Christ Jesus our
hope*. The word Saviour is not often used in the New Testament, but
is characteristic of the Pastorals (Pastorals, 10 times; 2 Peter, 5; rest of
the New Testament, 9). Sometimes it is applied to Christ (e.g. Tit.
2:13), sometimes to God the Father (e.g. 1 Tim. 2:3; 4:10). It is
used in the latter sense here (though it would be not impossible to
translate, 'God our Saviour, even Christ Jesus our hope'; for Jesus
Christ as God cp. Introduction, pp. 24 f., and note on Tit. 2:13):
God is the source of our salvation, and it is in the hoped-for coming

3 When I was starting for Macedonia, I urged you to stay on
at Ephesus. You were to command certain persons to give up
4 teaching erroneous doctrines and studying those interminable

---

of Jesus Christ (6:14; 2 Tim. 2:10; 4:8) that this salvation will be
complete. Christian hope is not based on human achievements, or on
an imaginative conjecture about what God may do in the future,
but simply on the fact of Jesus Christ.

2   *Timothy*: see Introduction, pp. 9 f., 30 f. *True-born* would ordinarily
describe the legitimate son of his father; what is meant here is that *in
the faith*, as a Christian believer and preacher, Timothy is a trustworthy disciple, who believes and preaches as Paul did.

Grace, mercy, peace. The extension of the earlier greetings (see above)
may possibly reflect liturgical usage. If grace and mercy are to be
distinguished, the former will point to God's gracious activity in
Jesus (2 Tim. 1:9; Tit. 2:11), that is, in the past, mercy to his treatment of sinful men at the judgement (2 Tim. 1:18), that is, in the
future; but both, like peace also, have an immediate bearing upon
the Christian life in the present (1 Tim. 1:14, 16; 2 Tim. 1:16; Tit.
2:11). They have no source but God.

2. 1:3–20. CHARGE TO TIMOTHY

General instructions are here mingled with the apostle's
charge to his disciple, just as later in the Epistle personal notes
and pieces of advice will be combined with Church regulations
(e.g. 3:14 ff.); but the general drift of the paragraph is that
of a personal commission (especially vv. 18 f.). Timothy's responsibility to keep his own teaching pure and sound naturally
carries with it the duty of driving away strange doctrines such
as those concerned with *interminable myths and genealogies*
(v. 4) and the *law* (v. 7). Over against these errors the true faith
is set forth in a 'faithful saying' (*words you may trust*, v. 15),
which gains force from its context, which narrates the conversion
of the persecutor, Paul. This paragraph (vv. 12–17) has at first
sight the appearance of a digression, but in fact it serves not
only to introduce the 'faithful saying' as a counterpart to the
errors combated, but also to supply the basis for Timothy's own
ministry.

3, 4   Timothy's first duty is to put a stop to heretical teaching at
Ephesus.

3   Paul first visited *Ephesus*, for a short time, on his way from Corinth

myths and genealogies, which issue in mere speculation and cannot make known God's plan for us, which works through faith.[1]

[1] *Or* cannot promote the faithful discharge of God's stewardship.

---

to Caesarea (Acts 18:19 ff.). He returned on his next journey (Acts 19:1), and remained in Ephesus about two years and three months (Acts 19:8, 10). At the end of this interval he set out for *Macedonia* (20:1; cp. 19:21). Acts records no further visit to Ephesus (cp. Acts 20:15–38, and note especially vv. 25, 38: 'None of you will see my face again'). It follows therefore that the present verse means either that when Paul left Ephesus (Acts 20:1) he asked Timothy to stay, or that he was released from imprisonment in Rome (Acts 28), travelled (not to Spain (Rom. 15:24, 28) but) again to the East, visiting Ephesus, and on some occasion leaving it once more for Macedonia. It is possible to find some support for the former alternative (see Introduction, p. 8), but the latter finds no support in the New Testament except in the Pastorals themselves, which alone bear witness to a first hearing of Paul's case (2 Tim. 4:16 f.), when he was rescued out of the lion's jaws.

Certain persons. The teachers of *erroneous doctrines* may well have included Hymenaeus and Alexander (v. 20); cp. 2 Tim. 2:17 (Hymenaeus and Philetus); also 2 Tim. 4:14. For their errors see the next verse and note; also Introduction, pp. 12–15; though it must not be assumed that all the false doctrines combated in the Pastorals were professed by the same teachers.

4   There are Christians in Ephesus who need to be warned *to give up . . . studying those interminable myths (μύθοις) and genealogies*. For myths cp. 4:7; 2 Tim. 4:4; Tit. 1:14 (also 2 Pet. 1:16); for genealogies cp. Tit. 3:9. In these passages the myths are described as godless, as fit only for old women, and as Jewish; with the genealogies they are said to issue in mere speculation, and are connected with controversies over the law. Some see here a reference to the myths used by the gnostics; the genealogies are then correspondingly taken to refer to the lists of emanations by means of which the gnostics sought to account for the creation of the world and the origin of the human race. Others, however, lay stress on the connexion asserted in the Pastorals themselves between myths and genealogies, and Judaism and the law; 'myths and genealogies' then becomes a term for speculative treatment of the Old Testament, referring specifically perhaps to stories of the creation, and other stories, respectively. There is no need to treat these views as alternatives. Colossians already bears witness to a combination of Judaism and gnosticism in a Christian heresy, and

5   The aim and object of this command is the love which
springs from a clean heart, from a good conscience, and from

---

the writings of Christian gnostics at a somewhat later time are full of
fanciful interpretation of the Old Testament (the Law). Even the
lists of emanations often reveal striking contacts with Old Testament
terms. That the new Christian faith provided a matrix for the fruitful
coming together of Jewish and Pagan ways of thinking is certainly
true; it is also true that as soon as the fusion ceased to be dominated
by Christian presuppositions the results were monstrous, and led to
anything but *God's plan* (οἰκονομίαν) *for us, which works through faith*.

Plan is used in the New Testament for God's universal plan of
salvation (Eph. 1:10; 3:2, 9), but it is here probably used in the
narrower sense of a particular application of God's plan (cp. 1 Cor.
9:17; Col. 1:25) as it affects some person or group. Mythical speculation does not *promote the faithful discharge of God's stewardship* (see
margin); it only leads men into *speculation* (better, perhaps, 'disputes').

It is worth noting that the author directs his charge against the
false teachers not so much on the ground that their doctrine is un-
true as on the ground that it has unhealthy consequences in the moral
life of the community.

The translation of vv. 3, 4 charitably conceals a defective Greek
sentence, which begins, As I urged you to stay on . . . , but is never completed. It is possible to regard vv. 5–20 as a parenthesis, and to take
2:1 as a deferred apodosis, but better to suppose that the writer lost
the thread of his sentence, the bad effects of heresy suggesting to his
mind a new thought on the true goal of faith.

11   Heresy leads men to quarrels; Christianity leads them to love. One
deviation from the true faith is the over-valuing, or rather the misinterpreting, of the Law. There were some who in their ignorant folly
set themselves up as teachers of the Law; but the true, Christian, use
of the Law is different from what they supposed.

5   The *command* of this verse is probably wider than that implied in
v. 3; it means the divine requirement disclosed in the Gospel. That
which the command, or charge, is intended to elicit is described in a
phrase characteristic of the understanding of Christianity found in
the Pastorals; it is *love*, proceeding *from a clean heart, from a good conscience, and from faith that is genuine*. Each of these terms is (for our
author) a way of speaking of sincerity. For the 'clean heart' cp. 2 Tim.
2:22; the basic meaning is freedom from mixed motives in the
Christian profession. For the 'good conscience' cp. 1:19; 3:9 (in both
of these faith is also mentioned, as here); 2 Tim. 1:3; these passages
also speak of sincerity. For 'faith that is genuine' cp. 2 Tim. 1:5; also

6 faith that is genuine. Through falling short of these, some
7 people have gone astray into a wilderness of words. They set
out to be teachers of the moral law, without understanding
either the words they use or the subjects about which they
are so dogmatic.

8   We all know that the law is an excellent thing, provided we

---

1 Tim. 1:19; 3:9 referred to above. Love is repeatedly praised or
enjoined in the Pastorals (1 Tim. 1:14; 2:15; 4:12; 6:11; 2 Tim.
1:7, 13; 2:22; 3:10; Tit. 2:2, (10)), doubtless because the writer was
aware of its centrality in the Christian life (cp., e.g., Mark 12:29 ff.;
Rom. 13:8 ff.; 1 Cor. 13:1–13), no doubt also because he was aware
of perversions of Christianity which made a show of piety, but were
loveless. It would be wrong to read a great depth of theological content into the terms used here. To have a good conscience, for example,
does not mean to be totally unaware of sin (which is scarcely a
Christian virtue), but simply not to practise conscious dissimulation
in religion.

6   The true goal of the Christian faith has too often been missed (the
word ἀστοχεῖν, here translated 'to fall short', is perhaps better rendered at 6:21, 'to shoot wide'; but its use in the Pastorals—1 Tim.
1:6; 6:21; 2 Tim. 2:18—suggests wilful error rather than unfortunate lack of success), and not love but only *a wilderness of words*
has been achieved (cp. Tit. 1:10; 3:9). Nothing grieves our author
more than a religion which is mere talk; see 1 Tim. 1:4, 7; 4:2, 7; 6:4,
20; 2 Tim. 2:16, 23; 3:5, 7; 4:4; Tit. 1:10, 14, 16; 3:9. He writes out
of knowledge of pious chatterers who represented themselves as
7 *teachers of the moral* (this adjective is not in the Greek) *law*; cp. Tit. 1:14.
There must have been a Jewish element in the false teaching combated here, but this need not be inconsistent with the view that the
error was fundamentally gnostic; see Introduction, pp. 13 f.

These self-appointed teachers of the Law do not know what they
are talking about. V. 7b as it stands in the translation is somewhat
repetitive; but *the subjects about which* (περὶ τίνων) could be 'the persons
about whom' (taking τίνων to be masculine), and in view of vv. 9 f.
it might be better to take it so: they talk about the Law, but apply
it to the wrong persons.

8–10   *The law is an excellent thing* (cp. Rom. 7:12), but it must be treated
as law, literally, 'lawfully'. This probably means 'correctly', 'in the
right way', the word 'lawfully' (νομίμως) being used in order to make
a verbal play on 'law' (νόμος). It is doubtful whether the distinction of
vv. 9 f. would have been made by Paul, to whom the law was the

9 treat it as law, recognizing that it is not aimed at good citizens,
but at the lawless and unruly, the impious and sinful, the
irreligious and worldly; at parricides and matricides, mur-
10 derers and fornicators, perverts, kidnappers, liars, perjurers
—in fact all whose behaviour flouts the wholesome teaching
11 which conforms with the gospel entrusted to me, the gospel
which tells of the glory of God in his eternal felicity.

---

command of God, which applied to *good citizens* as well as to *the lawless
and unruly, the impious and sinful, the irreligious and worldly*, and had the
effect of exposing the whole world to the judgement of God (Rom.
3:19); but the difference means only that our author is dealing with
law on a different level, and in a different context; we may perhaps
add, under the influence of Hellenistic thought, which also is aware
of the notion that good men need no law. The professed 'teachers of
the law' probably (*a*) spun out of it allegorical meanings which bore
no relation to the original sense, and (*b*) made it the basis of an ascetic
system of morals (cp. 4:3). Against this, it is here insisted that the
plain use of the law is for the 'restraining of wickedness and vice'; it
provides for a quiet and godly life, and if Christians are already living
such a life the law does not apply to them—its goal has already been
achieved.

10   The list of sinners involves what has been rightly called a 'Hellenistic transformation of Jewish ethics' (Dibelius–Conzelmann, p. 20).
The several terms do not need comment.

The wholesome teaching (ὑγιαινοῦσα διδασκαλία) is a phrase characteristic of the Pastorals (2 Tim. 4:3; Tit. 1:9; 2:1; for διδασκαλία
and διδαχή (teaching) cp. 1 Tim. 4:1, 6, 13, 16; 5:17; 6:1, 3; 2 Tim.
3:10, 16; 4:2, 3; Tit. 1:9; 2:1, 7, 10; for ὑγιαίνειν and ὑγιής [(to be)
healthy] cp. 1 Tim. 6:3; 2 Tim. 1:13; 4:3; Tit. 1:9, 13; 2:1, 2, 8).
Clearly it refers to the orthodox faith, but the words chosen to express
this are significant: *teaching* plays a large part in Church life, and
healthiness provides an admirable metaphor for the clean and energetic
wholeness of Christian life inculcated in these Epistles.

11   It is not clear how v. 11 is attached to what precedes. In the translation it is taken closely with *the wholesome teaching*; but 'in conformity
with (κατά) the gospel' could be taken as authenticating the teaching
just given about the proper use of the law. Possibly the best suggestion
is that the phrase is, grammatically, loosely attached (our author's
use of κατά cannot be called precise) to the paragraph as a whole: love
based on a pure heart, a good conscience, and genuine faith, is *in*

12   I thank him who has made me equal to the task, Christ
      Jesus our Lord; I thank him for judging me worthy of this
13   trust and appointing me to his service—although in the past
      I had met him with abuse and persecution and outrage. But

---

conformity with the gospel; the condemnation of misuse of the law is *in
conformity with the gospel;* the condemnation of fornication, lying, and
the like is also *in conformity with the gospel.* 'The gospel' is thus a
summary of Christian doctrine, proclamation, and teaching. This is
not the most characteristic Pauline use, but is not inconsistent with, for
example, Rom. 2:16.

   The gospel which tells of the glory of God could be rendered 'the
glorious gospel . . .', but in Greek which shows little sign of Semitism
there is no need to take the genitive in this way. 'The prime theme . . .
of the gospel is the glory of God' (C. H. Dodd, *History and the Gospel*
(1938), p. 36). We may well continue the quotation: 'But the glory
of God resides not in the static perfection of his being, but in his
mighty works.' God's *eternal felicity* is not (after the Greek pattern) a
self-regarding bliss. This gospel of the redemptive glory of God was
entrusted to me; this was what made Paul an apostle (1:1). This observation leads to the next paragraph.

12-17   Paul's appointment as an apostle was a signal instance of the grace
      of Christ, which is shown to have unique and permanent value as an
      example, and leads to a doxology.

12   This verse expands the 'entrusted to me' of v. 11. Paul's appoint-
      ment was based upon the Lord's foreknowledge that he would be a
      faithful servant (*worthy of this trust;* it would be possible to take the
      Greek to mean 'he considered me to be (already) a faithful person and
      therefore appointed me', but this is far less probable), and included a
      bestowal of power for the tasks he would have to perform: he *has
      made me equal to the task.* No task is specified; the thought of apostle-
      ship is in mind, and apostleship means *service*, ministry (διακονία; the
      word is certainly not used in a technical sense, but calls to mind the
      truth that there is no office in the Church, even the most exalted, that
      does not consist in serving rather than in being served; cp. Mark
      10:41–45).

13   For the *abuse, persecution, and outrage* which Paul had vented upon
      Christ and the Church, cp. Acts 7:58; 8:1, 3; 9:1, 13, 21; 22:4, 19;
      26:10 f.; 1 Cor. 15:9; Gal. 1:13; Phil. 3:6. This verse, superficially
      read, suggests that Paul's sins were pardoned because he *acted ignorantly*,
      just as v. 16 might similarly be taken to mean that his pardon was
      simply, or mainly, an example. If this were the full meaning of our
      Epistle it would be not merely (as is often said) inferior to but incon-

because I acted ignorantly in unbelief I was dealt with
14 mercifully; the grace of our Lord was lavished upon me,
with the faith and love which are ours in Christ Jesus.

15   Here are words you may trust, words that merit full

---

sistent with the doctrine of the New Testament as a whole; in fact,
as the context, and other passages in the Pastorals, show clearly, the
doctrine of grace assumed here is as rich as in the genuine Pauline
letters: Christ Jesus came into the world to save sinners (v. 15; not
those who unfortunately happened to be ignorant); cp. 2 Tim. 1:9;
Tit. 3:4–7. Paul's ignorance and unbelief, and the example he was to
show to later generations, form as it were the context in which his
forgiveness took place and became operative, and thus give to it a
special significance. These verses, however, are open to misinterpretation, and it is very difficult to believe that Paul himself wrote them.

4   Another verse only partially Pauline, in its somewhat imprecise use
of terms. For *the grace of our Lord was lavished* (ὑπερεπλεόνασεν) *upon me*
we may compare Rom. 5:20; but the connexion of this clause with
with the faith and love . . . is not clear. *Faith* must be the God-created
response in Paul himself (cp. v. 12, *worthy of this trust*); whether *love*
is God's love (parallel to *grace*), or responsive love to God, can hardly
be settled. If the latter, it should be noted that it is *in Christ Jesus*, that
is, it is not an independent human attitude, but one called into being
in Christ.

5   *Here are words you may trust* (πιστὸς ὁ λόγος) is a phrase used four
times in the Pastorals and nowhere else in the New Testament (1 Tim.
1:15; 4:9; 2 Tim. 2:11; Tit. 3:8; see also 1 Tim. 3:1, with the marginal alternative and the note). It marks out important formulations
of Christian belief and practice. Here, as at 4:9, it is reinforced by the
addition of *words that merit full acceptance* (or perhaps, '. . . are worthy
to be accepted by all'). The 'faithful saying' of this verse—*Christ Jesus
came into the world to save sinners*—is to be set against the common
charge that the Pastorals represent a moralizing kind of Christianity
(cp. to the same effect 1 Tim. 2:4 ff.; 3:16; 4:10; 2 Tim. 1:9 f.;
2:8, 10–13; 3:15; Tit. 2:11; 3:4–7). It is true that the author is
sensitive to the necessity of matching Christian profession with
Christian life and conduct, but he is confident that these are entirely
dependent upon God's gracious initiative in sending his Son as
Saviour, and an appropriation of this which depends in no way upon
human works (cp., e.g., Tit. 3:5) but entirely upon God (cp., e.g.,
2 Tim. 1:9). For the meaning of salvation in the Pastorals see further
Introduction, pp. 21–24.

acceptance: 'Christ Jesus came into the world to save sinners';
16 and among them I stand first. But I was mercifully dealt with
for this very purpose, that Jesus Christ might find in me the
first occasion for displaying all his patience, and that I might
be typical of all who were in future to have faith in him and
17 gain eternal life. Now to the King of all worlds, immortal,
invisible, the only God, be honour and glory for ever and
ever! Amen.

18 This charge, son Timothy, I lay upon you, following that

Among them I stand first is clearly a personal addition to the 'faithful
saying'; cp. 1 Cor. 15:9; 2 Cor. 12:11; Eph. 3:8.

16 *For this very purpose*: cp. v. 13 and note. Jesus Christ shows *patience*
(cp. Rom. 2:4; 9:22; also 3:25 f.) in permitting his adversaries to
continue until he brings them to faith. His patience with the great
persecutor was a signal example of this, which should prevent any
from despairing of his mercy. The first (or chief) of sinners provided the
first (or chief) *occasion* of patience and mercy.

Eternal life: cp. 6:12; Tit. 1:2; 3:7. Sometimes *life* (ζωή) is used
alone, or with some other qualification (4:8; 6:19; 2 Tim. 1:1, 10).
1 Tim. 4:8 (*this life, the life to come*) is instructive for the meaning of
the word; it refers to a transformed moral life lived in this age, and
equally to the full realization of this transformed life in the age to
come.

17 Recollection of God's unprecedented mercy naturally leads to a
doxology. *The King of all worlds* (βασιλεὺς τῶν αἰώνων) might be better
rendered, 'the King of the ages', i.e. the eternal King. Elsewhere
the expression occurs only at Rev. 15:3 (where it is translated 'king
of the ages'; the marginal alternative represents a different, and less
probably correct, text), but the thought of God as the eternal king is
a theme that runs throughout the Bible (e.g. Judges 8:23; 1 Sam.
8:7; Ps. 74:12; Isa. 6:5; Jer. 10:10). 'Of the ages' includes the
meaning, 'King of this age, and King of the age to come'. Not only in
the future, when his reign will be manifest, but also in the present,
when his reign is concealed (*invisible*), God is king.

Immortal (cp. Rom. 1:23), *invisible* (cp. Col. 1:15; Heb. 11:27),
only (cp. John 5:44; 17:3; Rom. 16:27; 1 Tim. 6:15 f.; Jude 4, 25;
Rev. 15:4), between them signify that God is truly God and not man.
To him alone *honour and glory* are due.

18–20 From the digression upon Paul's conversion and appointment, and
connected themes, the author returns to the special charge to Timothy,

prophetic utterance which first pointed you out to me. So
19 fight gallantly, armed with faith and a good conscience. It
was through spurning conscience that certain persons made
20 shipwreck of their faith, among them Hymenaeus and

---

which in the last verse becomes a specific warning against two named
persons.

18   *Charge*; cp. vv. 3, 5 (command). *I lay upon you*, or commit to you
($\pi\alpha\rho\alpha\tau i\theta\epsilon\mu\alpha\iota$), suggests a word and thought characteristic of the
Pastorals. A cognate noun ($\pi\alpha\rho\alpha\theta\acute{\eta}\kappa\eta$) occurs at 1 Tim. 6:20; 2 Tim.
1:12, 14; the verb (used here) at 2 Tim. 2:2 (translated, 'put into
the charge of'). It suggests that *charge* means more than a specific
injunction; it implies the responsibility laid upon Timothy by his
participation in the Christian faith, and indeed the faith itself (see
note on 6:20). This responsibility is metaphorically expressed in
terms of the warfare which Timothy must *fight gallantly*; cp. 2 Tim.
2:3 f., and 1 Tim. 6:12; 2 Tim. 4:7 (where different words are used).
Paul himself uses military metaphors (e.g. Rom. 6:13; 13:12; 1 Cor.
9:7; 2 Cor. 6:7; (Eph. 6:13–17); 1 Thess. 5:8), and they were
popular in the early Church. The thought of contending against evil
powers (1 Tim. 4:1; 6:12; 2 Tim. 2:26), and that of enduring the
rigours of a campaign (1 Tim. 6:8; 2 Tim. 2:3 f., 9; 3:12; 4:5), are
involved, as well as that of discipline.

    That prophetic utterance (literally, those prophetic utterances) *which
first pointed you out to me* must be compared with 4:14, which refers to
Timothy's ordination; also with Acts 13:1–3, where the Holy Spirit,
presumably through the prophets there mentioned, ordered the
separation of Paul and Barnabas to their mission in Asia Minor.
Timothy did not choose the ministry as a profession; he was marked
out for it by God. The translation rightly take the $\pi\rho o$- (before) in
$\pi\rho o\acute{\alpha}\gamma\epsilon\iota\nu$ in a spatial (not a temporal) sense; cp. R.V. margin (. . .
which led the way to thee); but the preposition also has its temporal
sense in so far as it emphasizes the divine initiative in calling to the
ministry.

19   *Armed with faith*; perhaps better, 'keeping faith', 'remaining faithful'.

    Good conscience; cp. v. 5. For those who are described as *spurning
conscience* cp. v. 6. The metaphor of *shipwreck* is not found elsewhere
in the New Testament.

    Their faith: in Greek faith ($\pi i\sigma\tau\iota s$) has the article and probably
means '*the* faith'—Christianity.

20   Two of the renegades are named: *Hymenaeus* (cp. 2 Tim. 2:17),
and *Alexander* (cp. 2 Tim. 4:14). It is possible to identify the latter
with the Alexander of Acts 19:33, but more probable that a different

Alexander, whom I consigned to Satan, in the hope that through this discipline they might learn not to be blasphemous.

2 First of all, then, I urge that petitions, prayers, intercessions,

---

man is intended in each place. It is important to consider these names in relation to the literary background of the Pastorals. There are three possibilities. (1) The names are purely fictitious, and were added in order to lend verisimilitude to the presentation of the material in the form of a personal letter from Paul to a disciple. (2) The present verse (if no more) was written by Paul himself; Hymenaeus and Alexander were men with whom he himself had had trouble. (3) Hymenaeus and Alexander belong to the true setting of the Pastorals, and were causing trouble in the Church at the time (after Paul's death) when the Pastorals were written. It is difficult to think that the two names were incorporated into 1 Timothy for no practical purpose, and for this reason (3) may be at least tentatively preferred; but we cannot identify Hymenaeus and Alexander, or use them to identify the setting of the Pastorals.

Whoever they were, Paul *consigned* them *to Satan*; cp. 1 Cor. 5:5. This passage, and the present, both suggest that some kind of, perhaps bodily though supernaturally inflicted, punishment is thought of (cp. perhaps 1 Cor. 11:30), with reformatory effect—*that through this discipline they might learn not to be blasphemous*, that is, in their erroneous teaching, which wrongs God by making false statements about him.

3. 2:1–6:21. THE ORDERING OF CHRISTIAN LIFE

After the opening chapter, which strikes a personal note, the Epistle turns to more general regulations for the ordering of Christian life, with special reference to the life of the community. The personal tone is not lost; the author can still use both the first and the second person singular; but even allusions to his own movements (3:14 f.; 4:13), and advice specifically directed to Timothy (3:15; 4:6 f., 12–16; 5:21 ff.; 6:11–14, 20), seem to have a more than personal reference. The author's main concerns stand out clearly: the purity of the apostolic Gospel must be maintained (3:15 f.; 4:6–10; 6:20); all Christians must live in a manner appropriate to their calling and their social position (2:8–15; 3:15; 6:1 f., 17 ff.); the Church's ministers must be sound in faith and practice (3:1–13; 5:1–22),

2 and thanksgivings be offered for all men; for sovereigns and all in high office, that we may lead a tranquil and quiet life in full observance of religion and high standards of morality.

---

and the whole Church must close its ranks against error and immorality (4:1–5; 6:3–10); Timothy himself must be an example in all respects. These interests give to the main body of the Epistle an underlying unity, though it is not always possible to find clear links between the paragraphs.

3a. **2:1–7.** PUBLIC PRAYER. *First of all* might be rendered 'Most important of all'; but whichever translation is adopted the words mean that the general regulation of Church life, for which the Epistle was written, begins at this point. Significantly it begins with the theme of prayer, though this is interrupted by a digression (vv. 4–7), after which renewed reference to prayer (v. 8) forms the link with what follows. The Church is a praying community.

1 *I urge*; here scarcely more, perhaps, than 'ask'.

If clear distinctions are to be made, *prayers* refers to man's approach to God in general (it is not clear why the word should stand second); *petitions* suggests man's requests on his own behalf, *intercessions* his requests on behalf of others; *thanksgivings* corresponds to intercessions —men's needs call for intercession, the benefits they enjoy for thanksgiving. *For all men* (note the stress on *all* in this paragraph) need not mean anything more precise than 'in respect of all men'; the different nouns which precede suggest different applications of the preposition (ὑπέρ).

2 That *sovereigns* (the plural simply generalizes, and does not mean that the Epistle was written at a time (after A.D. 137) when two men shared imperial authority) and their ministers (*all in high office*) should be prayed for was an accepted duty in Judaism (cp., e.g., Ezra 6:10; 1 Macc. 7:33; Philo, *In Flaccum* 49; *Pirqe Aboth* iii. 2); for the Christian attitude to the state compare especially Rom. 13:1–7; 1 Peter 2:13–17. Government is a good gift of God's providence, and Christians should pray for those who practise it, that what God intends by it should be achieved. This intention is described in the following words: *that we may lead a tranquil and quiet life in full observance of religion and high standards of morality.* The principal words in this sentence are all characteristic of the Pastorals: for 'tranquil and quiet' cp. vv. 11 f.; for 'religion' (εὐσέβεια), 3:16; 4:7, 8; 5:4; 6:3, 5, 6, 11; 2 Tim. 3:5, 12; Tit. 1:1; 2:12 (cp. 1 Tim. 2:10); for 'high standards of

3 Such prayer is right, and approved by God our Saviour,
4 whose will it is that all men should find salvation and come to

---

morality' (σεμνότης), 3:4, 8, 11; Tit. 2:2, 7. 'Tranquil and quiet' and
'morality' undoubtedly point to the outward conduct of the Christian
life; in these Epistles the Christian is a staid rather than an emotional
figure. The author was probably well aware of the dangerous excesses
into which a spiritual and enthusiastic religion could lead. Partly for
this reason it has been supposed that 'religion' also refers to the
appropriate conduct of the Christian life, though it has more often
been taken to denote the relation of the Christian (not to his fellow-
men but) to God, determined by grace and faith. It seems unnecessary
to treat these two interpretations as mutually exclusive alternatives.
A proper relation of man to God issues in suitable behaviour; har-
monious human relationships depend upon a correctly based relation
with God. Conversely, if (as is probably true) the author's thought
here as elsewhere has a controversial note, it is suggested that gnostic
theology and gnostic enthusiasm are bound up together. The object
of prayer for the state is that it may duly perform its divinely appointed task, so that Christians may practise Christianity as it ought
to be practised. Not only the danger of persecution, but also that of
attacks by demonic powers (cp. 2 Thess. 2:3–12) is in mind.

3 *Such prayer*; literally, 'This'. The pronoun probably refers both to
the offering of prayer, and to the tranquil progress of the Church,
which is the practical means by which men may find salvation and
come to know the truth (v. 4). *God our Saviour* in the context (see v. 6)
means probably God the Father rather than Jesus Christ; on the use
of the term Saviour in the Pastorals see note on 1:1, and Introduction,
pp. 24 f.

4 *Whose will it is that all men should find salvation* is an attack upon the
gnostic view that a predetermined group of 'spiritual' men would
inevitably be saved, and another group of 'material' men inevitably
be damned. It is God's will that all, not a few only, should *come to
know* (come to knowledge, ἐπίγνωσις, epi-gnosis) *the truth*.

The theological difficulties of this verse are evident. If the Almighty
wills that all should be saved, then surely all will be saved; but it
would be difficult to accommodate this absolute universalism in the
teaching of the New Testament as a whole, which is well aware of the
fact that there are some who perish (e.g. 1 Cor. 1:18). How may
the difficulties be resolved? Spicq (ad loc.) stresses the verb used for
'will'—θέλειν, not βούλεσθαι. The former word denotes 'le désir du
cœur, un sentiment', whereas the latter would suggest 'un ordre
absolu'. It is God's 'antecedent will', his intention in creation, that all
should be saved, though in fact there are some whom, on account of

5 know the truth. For there is one God, and also one mediator
6 between God and men, Christ Jesus, himself man, who sacrificed himself to win freedom for all mankind, so providing,

---

their sin, he necessarily condemns. Others have emphasized the use
of the passive infinitive (σωθῆναι, 'to be saved'); if the author had
written, 'God wills to save all men', then as the result of his irresis-
tible will all would have been saved; but 'to be saved' implies co-
operation on man's part (this is perhaps over-emphasized by the
translation '*find* salvation'), since man must consent to be saved,
and where his consent is wanting God's will is frustrated. Calvin
(*Institutes*, III. xxiv. 16; and ad loc.) rightly points out that the words
must be taken in their context. The author has just enjoined that
prayers be offered on behalf of sovereigns and high officials, and indeed for all men. This might well have seemed (in the circumstances
of the early Church) a fruitless activity, but in fact (the writer urges)
no class of men, even the most unlikely, such as kings, can be excluded
a priori from God's saving purpose. No difficulty arises if we can combine the notions of universal salvation and an elective process by regarding the latter as the means by which the former is realized (cp.
K. Barth, *Church Dogmatics*, II. i (1957), 508).

5   To all men (v. 4) correspond the *one God* and the *one mediator between
God and men*. The universal scope of the one way of salvation is
grounded in the fact that there is one God (cp. Rom. 3:29, where
Paul uses a similar argument to establish the parity of Jews and
Gentiles), and one means only by which men may come to him
(contrast the many intermediaries of the gnostic systems). The word
'mediator' is characteristic in the New Testament of Hebrews
(8:6; 9:15; 12:24), but is there used in a slightly different sense:
Jesus is the mediator of a new covenant, that is, the person through
whom, by whose agency, the new covenant is established. In 1
Timothy the point is rather that Jesus is a personal go-between who
enables men to come to God. He *himself* is *man*: this statement is to be
read in the light of the assertion, also found in the Pastorals, that
Jesus Christ is God (Tit. 2:13). Perhaps the writer feels that the pre-
dicate God is sufficiently contained in the name Christ Jesus, and
that it is Christ's manhood that calls for explicit mention here; more
probably, *man* is contrasted with the angelic (that is, neither truly
divine nor truly human) mediators believed in by gnostic heretics.
See further note on the next verse.

6   The universal availability of salvation is accounted for by the unity
of God; it is also rooted in the universal act of redemption performed
by the Mediator. As man, he offered himself on behalf of mankind
as a whole (ὑπὲρ πάντων). He *sacrificed himself to win freedom for all*

7 at the fitting time, proof of the divine purpose; of this I was
appointed herald and apostle (this is no lie, but the truth), to
instruct the nations in the true faith.

---

mankind is a free rendering of words which might be more literally
translated, '. . . gave himself as a ransom (ἀντίλυτρον) on behalf of all'.
This word for ransom occurs nowhere else in the New Testament
(and probably not in the Greek Old Testament); but the shorter
form (λύτρον) occurs at Mark 10:45 (= Matt. 20:28); cp. also
Tit. 2:14. It is true that the Christianity of the Pastorals has a strong
moral interest, but it rests as firmly as that of any part of the New
Testament upon a divine act of redemption. The goal of redemption
is the obtaining of freedom, but in a context which has already spoken
of Christ as the Mediator more stress is laid than the present translation brings out upon the transaction by which freedom is won. It
would indeed be mistaken to press the metaphor of ransom too far
(as, for example, by asking to whom the ransom-price was paid), but
it should nevertheless not be overlooked that this verse represents
Christ the Mediator as performing on men's behalf, and by means
of his death (he *sacrificed himself*), an act they could not perform for
themselves.

So providing, at the fitting time, proof of the divine purpose is a paraphrase,
probably correct, of an obscure phrase. Christ's act in 'giving himself' is described as a testimony; this should probably be understood
in the light of passages such as Rom. 5:8; his death was an objective
act of redemption, and at the same time a demonstration of God's
love for men, and of his will that they should be saved.

7   It is of this testimony or demonstration that Paul *was appointed
herald and apostle*. For 'apostle' see note on 1:1. This word is very
common in the New Testament; 'herald' (κῆρυξ), however, occurs
only here and in the very similar passage 2 Tim. 1:11 (and at 2 Pet.
2:5, where it is applied to Noah)—a surprising fact in view of the very
common New Testament use of the cognate verb, 'to herald' (i.e.
'to proclaim', 'to preach'; κηρύσσειν), and of the use of the noun to
describe philosophical missionaries such as Epictetus. The best explanation of this curious fact is that, according to Greek custom, the
person of a herald was inviolable; it was not so with the apostles (see
G. Friedrich in *T.W.N.T.* iii. 695). The word of God was not bound
(2 Tim. 2:9), but its preachers often were. Moreover, it was in their
message, not in their persons, that authority and importance resided.
The use of *herald* here, with *apostle*, lays stress on the evangelistic
aspect of the apostolic office. The word 'teacher' (*to instruct* represents
the Greek noun) is not intended to describe an office (cp. Acts 13:1;

8   It is my desire, therefore, that everywhere prayers be said
by the men of the congregation, who shall lift up their hands

---

1 Cor. 12:28; Eph. 4:11), but to indicate another aspect of Paul's
apostolic work. The writer of the Epistle (who may possibly be using
Pauline material in some form) knows that Paul's apostolic work was
carried on among the Gentiles (*nations*; cp. Rom. 11:13; 15:16;
Gal. 2:9), and he expresses its sphere as 'faith and truth' (possibly, as
taken in the translation, a hendiadys: *the true faith*).

A vehement asseveration of truthfulness (in the Pauline manner;
cp. Rom. 9:1; 2 Cor. 11:31; Gal. 1:20) is added: *this is no lie, but the
truth.*

3b. 2:8–15. THE PLACE OF WOMEN. The writer has already
called for prayer as the primary
obligation of the Church (v. 1).
This led to a digression (vv. 4–
7), but he now returns to the
main point, recognizing, however, that his requirement cannot be applied in the same way
to both male and female members of the Church. Men and
women are called equally to the
service of God; but they are not
called to precisely the same service.

8   *It is my desire* expresses a firm and
definite wish—almost an order.
The remainder of the verse expresses not the content (cp. vv. 1 f.
above) but the manner of the
prayers which *the men of the congregation* are to offer. (*a*) They are to
*lift up their hands with a pure inten-
tion*, literally, to 'lift up holy hands'.
To pray with uplifted hands was
the common practice in antiquity
(pagan, Jewish, and Christian); the
cleanliness which common decency
would suggest should be expres-

Detail from a third-century Christian sarcophagus, showing a praying figure with uplifted hands (1
Tim. 2:8).

sive of inward purity of intention and devotion. (*b*) *Angry or quarrelsome*

with a pure intention, excluding angry or quarrelsome
9 thoughts. Women again must dress in becoming manner,
modestly and soberly, not with elaborate hair-styles, not

---

thoughts are to be excluded. Appeal to the mercy of God cannot suitably
be made by men who are in themselves and their own dealings the
reverse of merciful.

Such prayer is to be made *everywhere*, better 'in every place' (ἐν
παντὶ τόπῳ). This is no mere literalism, for in Jewish usage 'place'
meant 'meeting-place', 'place of prayer', and there is evidence
(especially 1 Cor. 1:2; 1 Thess. 1:8) that it became Christian usage
too. The author means 'in every Christian meeting-place'. Cp. also
Mal. 1:10 f.

No detailed instructions are given about the conduct of meetings
for prayer. Apparently all male members of the Church had an equal
right to offer prayer, and were expected to use their right. There is no
mention of a president who acts on behalf of the congregation. But

'. . . not with elaborate hair-styles' (1 Tim. 2:9). A third-century relief from
Trier shows four maids at work on a lady's toilet.

10 decked out with gold or pearls, or expensive clothes, but
with good deeds, as befits women who claim to be religious.
11 A woman must be a learner, listening quietly and with due
12 submission. I do not permit a woman to be a teacher, nor

---

9 *women* have a different role, though they too receive a similar injunction (*again*, rendering ὡσαύτως). The sentence (vv. 9 f.) contains no
main verb, and it is best to supply from v. 8 the verb 'to pray', so
that the translation will be, 'In the same way, I desire that women
should pray, dressed *in becoming manner* . . .'. Men will pray aloud, with
outward gesture; women also will pray, but with care not to draw
10 attention to themselves. For a *religious* (the word is characteristic of
the Pastorals; cp. v. 2 above—here the word is θεοσέβεια) woman
the proper adornment consists of *good deeds*. These good deeds, which
are very often mentioned in the Pastorals (1 Tim. 5:10, 25; 6:18
(cp. 3:1); 2 Tim. 2:21; 3:17; Tit. 1:16; 2:7, 14; 3:1, 8, 14), are
not to be confused with the works of law rejected by Paul as a ground
of justification (e.g. Rom. 3:28), and rejected with equal vehemency
in the Pastorals (2 Tim. 1:9). They are the outcome of, not a pre-
liminary condition of or substitute for, Christian faith.

There is no question here or elsewhere in the New Testament that
women have equal standing with men in Christ, in whom there is
neither male nor female (Gal. 3:28). This proposition of Paul's, however, does not mean that, among Christians, the distinguishing
characteristics of the sexes are obliterated, nor does it mean that in
their relations with others, and in the public assemblies of the Church,
women should do exactly the same things as men. We shall see first
the role ascribed to women by our author, and then the grounds on
which he bases his statement.

12 A woman must (*a*) learn and not teach; (*b*) not *domineer over man*
(better perhaps, 'over her husband'); (*c*) *be quiet*; (*d*) maintain her
due place (this is better than *with due submission*). For these instructions cp. 1 Cor. 11:3–16; 14:34 f. These two passages (within the same
Epistle) are sufficient to show that in the apostolic (and indeed in the
Pauline) churches, practice was not uniform. Sometimes the difference
between man and woman was best expressed by woman's complete
silence; sometimes by her dress. The author of the Pastorals has no
doubt that in the circumstances of his own time silence should be the
rule; it may not be wrong to connect this with the 'godless myths,
fit only for old women' (4:7). Women were apt to do too much talking, and that of the wrong kind (cp. 3:11; 5:13). Compare perhaps
also 4:3, 'they forbid marriage': this ascetic principle, which the
Pastorals reject, could more easily lead to the domineering woman

13 must woman domineer over man; she should be quiet. For
14 Adam was created first, and Eve afterwards; and it was not
Adam who was deceived; it was the woman who, yielding to
15 deception, fell into sin. Yet she will be saved through motherhood[1]—if only women continue in faith,[2] love, and holiness,
with a sober mind.

---

[1] *Or* saved through the Birth of the Child, *or* brought safely through childbirth.   [2] *Or* if only husband and wife continue in mutual fidelity . . .

---

than the family life, which the Pastorals regard as ideal for women.
For the 'quietness' enjoined here cp. v. 2; it is not for women only.
See further note on 3:11.

The regulations governing the actions of women in public are
dictated by practical considerations, but their relation to men rests
on more fundamental grounds, which belong to the created order
itself. Adam was first in creation, Eve in sin. The author is dependent
13, 14   upon the narrative of Gen. 2 f. Adam was created by God (Gen. 2:7),
and Eve made from one of Adam's ribs (Gen. 2:21 ff.). It was
Eve whom the serpent approached (Gen. 3:1), and Eve who first
ate the forbidden fruit (Gen. 3:6). In both respects, the resemblance
between the man and the woman is much greater than the difference.
It is not, and cannot be, denied that the woman was created by God,
or that the man fell into sin. The difference is a matter of priority.

15   The next verse is very obscure. The subject of *will be saved* must
be *the woman* of v. 14; but whether in the sense of Eve, or of woman
in general, is not clear. It is surprising to meet in the second clause a
plural verb: *if* they *continue*. No subject is expressed in the Greek;
we must understand *women* (corresponding to the generalized use
of 'woman' derived from v. 14), or possibly (with the margin)
husband and wife, or even '(the woman's) children'. There is further am-
biguity in *will be saved*, which might describe salvation in a religious
sense, or physical preservation; and in 'childbirth' (the rendering *motherhood* seems baseless except as a euphemism), which might
refer to the bearing of children by any woman, or to the bearing
of Jesus by Mary, the new Eve. Complete assurance in settling
these alternatives is not to be had, but decisive considerations seem
to be (1) that though Eve is mentioned the passage as a whole
(vv. 9–15) is about woman in general, and (2) that the author's view
is that woman's vocation is not to public life but to the task of bearing
and bringing up children (v. 12; 1 Tim. 5:10, 14; Tit. 2:2–5). With
these facts in mind we may paraphrase: In consequence of her place

3   There is a popular saying:[1] 'To aspire to leadership is an
2 honourable ambition.' Our leader, therefore, or bishop,

[1] *Some witnesses read* Here are words you may trust, *which some interpreters*
attach to the end of the preceding paragraph.

---

in creation, and of Eve's fall, woman is involved in distress and danger
(Gen. 3:16); nevertheless, she will be preserved through these, if they
(women; the change of number is a lapse, but one very easy to commit
in writing) continue as devout Christians. Reference to the husbands
or children of Christian women seems very remote, and reference to
Mary's bearing of Jesus still more so.

3c. **3:1–16.** THE QUALITIES REQUIRED IN MINISTERS. With 3:1
(on the opening words see below) the author turns to one of his
principal themes. On *leaders*, or *bishops* (vv. 1–7), and *deacons*
(vv. 8–13), see the notes below and Introduction, pp. 31 f. The
chapter ends with a brief doctrinal account of the reasons why
men should behave suitably (for example, in the conduct of
their ministry) in the Church of God.

1   The paragraph opens with the words, *There is a popular saying*. A
variant with much more numerous MS. support is, 'Here are words
you may trust' (cp. 1:15 and note). If this alternative is accepted, the
words may be an introduction to what follows; since, however, the
sentence that follows is scarcely of the same kind as the other 'words
you may trust' they may more appropriately be attached to the preceding sentence (2:15; for this backward reference cf. 4:8 f.; Tit.
3:8). There would be a natural inclination on the part of copyists to
substitute the common phrase (πιστὸς ὁ λόγος) for the uncommon
(ἀνθρωπινὸς ὁ λόγος); but the better attested text, with the comment
attached to the foregoing verse, is perhaps the better reading, and
might have been changed into that adopted in the translation because
3:1b seemed an odd 'faithful saying'.

By 'popular', the author (or corrector, if the marginal reading be
preferred) probably means 'in general (i.e. not only Christian) use';
the list of virtues which follows is probably not of Christian origin,
and the word (ἐπισκοπή) translated 'leadership' may in non-Christian
usage have meant simply 'office', 'position'. Men needed encouragement to seek secular office, which was often arduous and expensive,
and won little gratitude; the office of a Christian minister was, from
the worldly point of view, even less attractive.

2 *Our leader ... or bishop* translates one word (ἐπίσκοπος) which was in process of becoming a technical term. For its use in the Pastorals see Introduction, p. 32; and for the present passage cp. Tit. 1:7 ff. The word *episkopos* has a considerable pre-Christian background as well as a long Christian history. The most important points are as follows: (1) In non-biblical Greek the word is used in a variety of more or less technical senses to describe functions exercised by both gods and men (see H. W. Beyer in *T.W.N.T.* ii. 605–10). Sometimes the function is financial, occasionally religious; most important perhaps is the use of the word (and cognates) to denote the Cynic-Stoic missionary preacher of righteousness (cp. 'herald' at 2:7). The *episkopos* is a leader, or overseer. (2) In the community known to us from the so-called Damascus Document and the Dead Sea Scrolls, there were officers bearing the title *meᵇbaqqer*; this is a reasonably close etymological equivalent of *episkopos*. The *meᵇbaqqer* is an interpreter of the law, a preacher and pastor, and the officer most closely concerned with the initiation of novices. (3) Most important of all is the background in the Old Testament, where the cognate verb (ἐπισκέπτεσθαι) is used to describe God's visiting his people to redeem them (also, on occasion, to punish); so, e.g., Exod. 4:31; 32:34. This third usage is primary in the use of *episkopos* at 1 Pet. 2:25; elsewhere in the New Testament the word occurs only at Acts 20:28, where it is clearly synonymous with πρεσβύτερος (presbyter, elder), and at Phil. 1:1 ('bishops and deacons'; there is much to be said for the view that here, as in some of the non-biblical material mentioned above, the office was primarily financial). In the Pastorals, *episkopos* seems to describe the theological function of ministers whose position in the community is otherwise given by the term 'elder'. It is hard on any other view to account for the absence of elders from the present chapter, and for Tit. 1:7. The further development of the term and of the office do not fall within the scope of this commentary.

The qualifications here laid down as requisite in leaders, or bishops, are almost exclusively moral; the author's primary concern is not to commend a particular pattern of ministry, but to insist that ministers should be good ministers.

Above reproach: to be understood literally, as of one against whom no charge can be brought. *Faithful to his one wife* is notoriously obscure (cp. 3:12; Tit. 1:6; cf. 1 Tim. 5:9); literally, 'husband of one wife'. The three possible interpretations are given in text and margin. 'Married to one wife' is an improbable interpretation; polygamy is unlikely to have been a serious danger. 'Married only once' implies a prohibition of second marriage after the death of the first wife. This is possible but (1) this kind of abstention if required at all would not be confined to leaders; (2) in 5:14 younger widows are enjoined to marry again. It may be urged that 'faithful to his one wife' would

must be above reproach, faithful to his one wife,[1] sober,
3 temperate, courteous, hospitable, and a good teacher; he
must not be given to drink, or a brawler, but of a forbearing
4 disposition, avoiding quarrels, and no lover of money. He
must be one who manages his own household well and wins
obedience from his children, and a man of the highest prin-
5 ciples. If a man does not know how to control his own family,
6 how can he look after a congregation of God's people? He
must not be a convert newly baptized, for fear the sin of

[1] *Or* married to one wife, *or* married only once.

---

equally be a requirement laid not upon leaders only but upon all
Christians; this argument, however, loses weight if the words are
quoted from a *popular* saying, describing the qualifications for public
office. Christian leaders must observe standards at least as high as
those looked for in secular office-bearers. *Hospitable*: cp. Tit. 1:8; also
Rom. 12:13; Heb. 13:2; 1 Pet. 4:9; a necessary and frequently emphasized virtue in early Christianity. *A good teacher*: cp. Tit. 1:9; also
1 Tim. 5:17. It seems that not all elders taught, but that it was de-
3 sirable that a leader should be able to do so. *No lover of money*: it is
doubtful whether an *episkopos* would as such receive much money,
but the position of responsibility (perhaps financial responsibility)
which he occupied would present opportunities for dishonest and
grasping behaviour; see the note above with reference to Phil. 1:1.
, 5 It is assumed that the leader, or bishop, will be a married man, and
a father. His ability to control his own family will bear witness to his
fitness for a responsible position in God's family. His work is to
manage, or *control*—these words both translate the same Greek word—
better, perhaps, 'to preside over'. He must be *a man of the highest
principles* (μετὰ πάσης σεμνότητος). σεμνότης is a word characteristic
of the Pastorals (1 Tim. 2:2; 3:4; Tit. 2:7; cp. σεμνός (the cognate
adjective), 1 Tim. 3:8, 11; Tit. 2:2). It describes the bearing of the
head of the family: seriousness, dignity, gravity.

The requirements so far made in these verses recall those made of
6 aspirants to secular office. *Not . . . a convert newly baptized* seems to be
more specifically Christian, both in itself, and in the warning attached,
which should probably be understood as in the margin. The devil
fell into *the sin of conceit*, and thus incurred judgement; one who had
risen too rapidly to leadership might fall into condemnation for the
same sin. The reading of the text (*a judgement contrived by the devil*) is

conceit should bring upon him a judgement contrived by the
7 devil.[1] He must moreover have a good reputation with the
non-Christian public, so that he may not be exposed to
scandal and get caught in the devil's snare.

8   Deacons, likewise, must be men of high principle, not in-
dulging in double talk, given neither to excessive drinking nor

----

[1] *Or* the judgement once passed on the devil.

----

grammatically possible; but judgement is not contrived by the devil
but carried out by God in strict accord with truth. Some see a reference here not to the devil (ὁ διάβολος—the slanderer *par excellence*),
but to a human slanderer. This is possible but, in the context, unlikely.
The next verse describes the devil's activity.

7   The leader or bishop must *have a good reputation with the non-Christian
public* (literally, 'those who are outside'; cp. Mark 4:11), which is
ready enough to oppose the Christian faith; there is no need to
multiply its opportunities by unnecessary *scandal*, in addition to the
necessary offence of the Cross. The *devil* is ready to catch men, and
especially new Christians, in his *snare*, which in their inexperience they
may fail to detect; clearly it would be particularly profitable for him
if he could succeed in catching a leader. Leaders should therefore be
men of experience.

8–13   The regulations for the office of deacon are closely parallel—*likewise*; cp. also v. 10—to those for bishops. Neither office can be simply
taken up without an inquiry into character. On *deacons* generally see
Introduction, pp. 31 f. In the New Testament the word appears very
seldom in a technical sense; see Phil. 1:1 (see above, note on v. 2;
probably at Philippi the deacons helped the bishops in financial and
eleemosynary affairs), and Rom. 16:1 (see below, note on v. 11). It
is wrong to add a reference to Acts 6; the seven men there appointed
are not described as deacons (διάκονοι). As a Greek word διάκονος
means simply 'servant', latinized as *minister*. Its significant background
lies exclusively in the New Testament, and like ἐπίσκοπος it is a Christological term; see especially Mark 10:45.

8   Deacons must be *men of high principle*; see note on v. 4. They must
not indulge in *double talk*. Not *given . . . to excessive drinking* is paralleled
in the rules for bishops (v. 3), though different words are used; again,
not *given . . . to money-grubbing* differs little from 'no lover of money'
(v. 3); the author is thinking less of dishonesty than of the sordidness
of using Christian office for financial profit. Moral and theological
requirements are summed up in the requirement that deacons should

9 to money-grubbing. They must be men who combine a clear
conscience with a firm hold on the deep truths of our faith.
10 No less than bishops, they must first undergo a scrutiny, and
11 if there is no mark against them, they may serve. Their wives,[1]
equally, must be women of high principle, who will not talk

[1] *Or* . . . serve. Deaconesses . . .

---

9 *combine a clear conscience* (cp. 1:5) *with a firm hold on the deep truths*
(literally, mystery; see v. 16) *of our faith.* In v. 13 as here translated it
appears that though preaching may not have been a major activity
of deacons they as well as elders did preach; hence the necessity for
intelligent as well as sincere faith. Even if a different view is taken of
v. 13 (see the notes) a sound theological understanding would be
called for in the pastoral work done by deacons.

10   *No less than bishops, they.* . . . A correct though paraphrasing interpretation of 'These also . . .'. Candidates for episcopal office must be
tested on the lines indicated in vv. 2–7; prospective deacons also. *If
there is no mark against them* corresponds to 'above reproach' (v. 2; see
note). How the testing was to be carried out is not said; most of the
qualities required would be matters of the candidate's known public
reputation. The letter-form implies that Timothy will supervise if he
does not actually conduct the scrutiny, but the regulations themselves are worded so as to be of more general application. This
corresponds with the intention of the Epistle, which is to provide a
pattern for the conduct of the Church as a whole.

11   *Their wives*; margin, *Deaconesses.* The Greek is ambiguous. In favour
of the rendering 'wives' are the following points: (1) vv. 8 ff. and 12 f.
deal with male deacons; it is unlikely that a reference to deaconesses
would be introduced between these small paragraphs; (2) a reference
to deaconesses would have been more detailed; for example, it might
have required that a deaconess be 'faithful to her one husband' (cp.
5:9); (3) a more explicit term than 'women' ($\gamma\upsilon\nu\alpha\hat{\imath}\kappa\epsilon\varsigma$) would have
been used; (4) the ministry of women is dealt with in 5:3–16, and
there women workers are 'widows'. On the other side the following
points have been made: (1) in New Testament times the word deacon
($\delta\iota\acute{\alpha}\kappa o\nu o\varsigma$) had no feminine (cp. Rom. 16:1), so that the author was
obliged to use some such word as 'women'; (2) v. 11 is grammatically
dependent upon v. 2, and, like v. 8, is introduced by the word
$\dot{\omega}\sigma\alpha\acute{\upsilon}\tau\omega\varsigma$ (this is obscured by the translation, which in v. 8 has 'likewise', in v. 11 *equally*), which indicates a new paragraph in a sequence
of rules for different groups of officials; (3) the virtues required (especially *women of high principle*, cp. vv. 4, 8) are eminently those of

12 scandal, sober and trustworthy in every way. A deacon must be faithful to his one wife,[1] and good at managing his chil-
13 dren and his own household. For deacons with a good record

---

[1] *Or* married to one wife, *or* married only once.

---

ministers; (4) if the author had referred to deacons' wives he would have been obliged to be more precise, by writing '*their* wives' (there is no possessive pronoun or article in the Greek, though a possessive pronoun is introduced into the translation), or by using a construction like that of v. 4 (γυναῖκας ἔχοντες). It cannot be said that either set of arguments is conclusive, but the latter is perhaps the stronger; and it may be well to note that, notwithstanding 2:9–12, women ministers were by no means unknown in the apostolic Church: cp. Prisca (or Priscilla; Acts 18:2, 18, 26; Rom. 16:3; 1 Cor. 16:19); Phoebe (described in Rom. 16:1 as a διάκονος, though here the word may not have its full technical sense); and various other women who helped or prophesied (e.g. Acts 1:14; 12:12; 16:15, 40; 21:9; Rom. 16:6, 12; 1 Cor. 11:5). Not far from the date of the Pastorals themselves note Pliny's reference to the two *ancillae quae ministrae dicebantur* (*Letters*, x. 96). These women, whether themselves office-holders or the wives of office-holders, are required to show fundamental Christian virtues. For *women of high principle* see note on v. 4; *scandal*—it would be easy both for deaconesses and for deacons' wives to talk more than they should; to avoid this they should be *sober* (cp. vv. 2, 8), and *trustworthy in every way* (cp. 1:12).

12   The author returns to male deacons; for his requirements here cp.
13 vv. 2, 4 f. Those who have passed the test and proved themselves in service *may claim a high standing and the right to speak openly on matters of the Christian faith*. The word 'standing' (βαθμός) signifies first, a step, then, rank, or degree. The adjective 'high' corresponds to the word (adverb, in Greek) used in *good record*. *Good* service leads to *good* standing; that is, in the community at large. It is possible that standing points to the opportunity of promotion (presumably to the office of elder-bishop); but this is far from certain. The translation takes the concluding clause to belong to the same context: in the community, the deacon with a good record may speak freely on matters of faith (in preaching, teaching, or informal group). This is supported by the original sense of the word παρρησία, which means 'freedom and boldness of speech'. The word, however, does not always retain this meaning in the New Testament, but not infrequently means 'confident approach to God' (so Eph. 3:12; Heb. (3:6); 4:16; 10:19, 35; 1 John 2:28; 3:21; 4:17; 5:14). It seems likely that it has this

of service may claim a high standing and the right to speak openly on matters of the Christian faith.

15   I am hoping to come to you before long, but I write this in case I am delayed, to let you know how men ought to conduct themselves in God's household, that is, the church of the

---

meaning here. The good deacon has not only a good standing with men, but a free and confident approach to God—not *because* he is a good deacon, but because as a good deacon he knows well the meaning of faith in Christ Jesus ('on matters of the Christian faith' is literally 'in faith which is in Christ Jesus').

16   The preceding paragraphs could be headed, 'How to conduct one-self in God's household'. The author has borrowed freely from non-Christian lists of virtues and qualifications, but the foundation of his exhortation is specifically Christian, and Christocentric. This is briefly developed by further quotation, from a Christian source.

14   Paul hopes to see Timothy *before long*, but he cannot be certain of
15   this; he may be *delayed* and therefore puts on paper the main substance of what he has to say. It is probably correct to see disclosed here the 'plot' of the Pastoral Epistles; Paul is now for ever absent, but he may nevertheless deal with the new situation; see Introduction, pp. 16 ff.

The Church is *God's household*. 'There are good reasons why God bestows this name on his Church; for not only has he received us to be his children by the grace of adoption, but he also dwelleth in the midst of us' (Calvin). The context (cp. v. 5) shows that in using the word οἶκος (house) the author is thinking of 'household'; but having used the word (which is as ambiguous in Greek as 'house' is in English) his thought turns in the direction of the building; the Church is also *the pillar and bulwark of the truth* (neither 'household' nor 'pillar and bulwark' has an article in Greek; it may be that the author is thinking of each local congregation as severally a pillar and bulwark). 'The truth' is regularly used in the Pastorals (1 Tim. 4:3; 6:5; 2 Tim. 2:15, 18; 3:8; 4:4; Tit. 1:14, and perhaps other passages) for the content of the Christian faith; probably it is so used here. But in what sense can the Church be 'the pillar and bulwark' of the truth—upon which it is itself founded? The answer is to be sought not so much in the activity of preaching (so Calvin), though this is important, as in defence against heresy. The heretics have 'lost grip of the truth' (1 Tim. 6:5), have 'shot wide of the truth' (2 Tim. 2:18), 'defy the truth' (2 Tim. 3:8), 'stop their ears to the truth' (2 Tim. 4:4), 'turn their backs upon the truth' (Tit. 1:14). Over against such men

16 living God, the pillar and bulwark of the truth. And great
beyond all question is the mystery of our religion:

> 'He who was manifested in the body,
> vindicated in the spirit,
> seen by angels;
> who was proclaimed among the nations,
> believed in throughout the world,
> glorified in high heaven.'

---

the Church will 'join the struggle in defence of the faith, the faith
which God entrusted to his people once and for all' (Jude 3), and
uphold it. To say this is not to make the truth dependent upon the
Church (though it may be questioned whether Paul would have
expressed himself in these somewhat ambiguous terms), but to represent the Church, in its members and ministers, as the servant of
the truth, or word, of God.

The picture of the Church as a building is common in the New
Testament; see Matt. 16:18; John 2:21; 1 Cor. 3:9–17; 6:19; Gal.
2:9 (the Church has its pillars); 4:26 (the heavenly Jerusalem);
Eph. 2:20 ff.; 1 Peter 2:3 ff.; Rev. 21:2; &c. The Pastorals are not
concerned (as several of these passages are) with the Church as the
heavenly city, or heavenly temple, appearing on earth in the last
days. The Church is an organism, and indeed an organization,
which stands firm against error, and it is important to know how to
conduct oneself in it (that is, within its organization, but also as a
member of it).

Nevertheless, it is the truth that matters most, because it is the
truth of *the living God*, to whom the Church belongs; and the truth,
16 described as *the mystery of our religion* (cp. 2:2), is set forth in what
appears to be a quotation from a hymn or creed:

> *He who was manifested in the body,*
> *vindicated in the spirit,*
> *seen by angels;*
> *who was proclaimed among the nations,*
> *believed in throughout the world,*
> *glorified in high heaven.*

Our translation casts the quotation in the form of two three-lined
strophes. This is possible but not necessary, since each of the six lines
is similar in form, and it is legitimate to arrange them as three couplets, or as six parallel single lines. There seems to be no decisive reason

why any of these arrangements should be preferred to the others (see, however, below). It has been suggested that the first three lines should be punctuated

> He who was manifested
> was justified in the body,
> appeared in the spirit to angels;

but in view of the general parallelism this seems unlikely. The opening words ('He who') are almost certainly correct, though there is considerable MS. support for 'God' and some for 'which'. The latter (ὅ, neuter relative pronoun) is a correction made by copyists who thought that the relative should agree with 'mystery' (neuter in Greek); the former (θεός, written contracted in uncials as $\overline{ΘC}$) was a natural corruption of 'he who' (OC). Most of this Christological summary is quite clear. The subject is Jesus Christ, who is man (1 Tim. 2:5), Saviour (2 Tim. 1:10), and God (Tit. 2:13). His pre-existence is assumed (cp. 2 Tim. 1:9). Difficulty lies only in the third and sixth lines, which may for the moment be deferred. The eternal Son of God was manifested in flesh (ἐν σαρκί; it is perhaps better to retain this word—the body in which Christ was manifested was in the fullest sense real and human, being composed of flesh). At the end of his earthly existence, he was vindicated when God raised him up after the death he had voluntarily endured. This was done 'in the spirit', not in that his flesh was not raised, but in that it was the Spirit (of God), not flesh in itself, which was capable of effecting resurrection. This is a common thought in the New Testament; cp. especially Rom. 1:4; 1 Peter 3:18; also John 6:63. This crucified and risen Person was proclaimed (as Lord and Saviour) not only among the Jews (to whom he had at first been manifested) but also among the Gentiles (this, as at 2:7, is probably a better rendering of ἔθνη; there is certainly an allusion to the work of Paul), and throughout the world the response of faith had been made. This last statement does not in itself imply a late date for the Epistle; cp. Rom. 15:19; Col. 1:6, 23.

The difficulty in lines 3 and 6 is that, though the hymn as a whole seems to follow a chronological sequence, these two lines seem at first to refer to the same event—the ascension (see Acts 1:9 ff.; Eph. 4:8 ff.; 1 Pet. 3:22), in which Christ was 'glorified in high heaven' (literally, 'received up in glory') and so returned to, and was presumably seen by, the angelic company in heaven. 'Seen by angels' may, however, have a different sense. It is an attractive suggestion that the noun (ἀγγέλοις) has its primary meaning, (not angels but) 'messengers'—that is, the apostolic witnesses of the resurrection. The verb (ὤφθη) is that used, for example, by Paul in this setting (1 Cor. 15:5–8). But 'angel' is too common a meaning of ἄγγελος to be lightly set aside. Another suggestion is that 'angels' refers to those inferior

4   The Spirit says expressly that in after times some will desert
from the faith and give their minds to subversive doctrines

---

and potentially evil spiritual beings whose rule was ended by the
death and resurrection of Jesus. It is true that in Paul, angels (and
kindred beings such as principalities, powers, and the like) are often
evil, or at least far from good. A third suggestion proceeds from 1 Pet.
1:12 ('These are things that angels long to see into'): the saving
events of the incarnation and resurrection were beheld by angels.

The sixth line may be taken as a simple reference to the ascension
if the third is understood as corresponding to a descent into Hades, to
deal with rebellious angels; or it may refer to the final enthronement
of Christ when all his foes have been defeated (1 Cor. 15:25; Phil.
2:10 f.).

On the whole it seems best to recognize a chronological progression
in the hymn (if such it is), and to suppose that it refers to (1) the incarnation, (2) the resurrection, (3) the ascension, (4) the preaching of
the Gospel, (5) the response to it, and (6) the final victory of Christ.
If the lines are to be grouped, it will be best to group them in pairs,
and to see them as leading to the enthronement as a climax (so Jeremias, ad loc.). (1) The King is *exalted* (in manifestation and vindica-
tion); (2) he is *presented* (to the heavenly and to the human world);
(3) he is enthroned (by the believing obedience of men, and in
heavenly glory). It is probable that the hymn rests in some degree on
pre-Christian models, but there is no question of its appropriateness,
in its present form, for celebrating in Christian terms the redemptive
acts of God in history. It is noteworthy that the proclamation of
Christ is included, along with the incarnation and resurrection, as
part of the redemptive history.

3d. **4:1–5.** THE GROWING PERIL OF FALSE DOCTRINE. Much of
the later part of the Epistle is devoted to advice given to Timothy
for the conduct of his ministry. It is set against a background
formed by the activity of heretics, who are not merely deluded
in their theological thinking but perverted in conscience; they
therefore debase the practice as well as the teaching of the
Church. On the general question of the false teaching presupposed by the Pastorals see Introduction, pp. 12–15; the
author regards it as an eschatological phenomenon (cp. 1 John
2:18; 4:1 ff.), foretold by Paul.

1   *The Spirit* is the Spirit of prophecy, and the prophets who have
foretold the apostasy described in this verse are Christian prophets;

2 inspired by devils, through the specious falsehoods of men
3 whose own conscience is branded with the devil's sign. They
forbid marriage and inculcate abstinence from certain foods,

---

cp. Mark 13:22; 2 Thess. 2:3, 11 f.; Acts 20:29 f.; Rev. 13. *In after times* is in Greek an expression similar to that translated 'the final age' (2 Tim. 3:1), and this is probably its meaning, though it means also 'after the time of Paul'. Before his final defeat, Satan makes a last attack upon the people of God by means of *subversive doctrines inspired by devils*. What these doctrines are appears shortly; the author is in no doubt of their origin. If he is still (as Paul was) conscious of living in the last times it is in a negative sense; he says, 'The world is so bad it cannot last much longer', rather than, 'It is far on in the night; day is near' (Rom. 13:12).

The men who thus lead others astray from *the faith* (note this clear example of the objective use of the term—*fides quae creditur*) are not
2 merely in error; the fault lies in their *conscience*, which is *branded with the devil's sign*. This translation reads a (probably correct) interpretation into the context, which contains no literal equivalent to the last four words. If, however, the Greek participle (κεκαυστηριασμένων) is translated 'branded', v. 1 plainly suggests whose brand has been given. It would be possible to translate 'seared'; the thought would then be that the consciences of the deceivers were past all feeling, and therefore ineffective. Their ideas of right and wrong have gone astray.

On the general problem of identifying the heretics referred to in the Pastorals see Introduction, pp. 12–15. It is clear from this passage that men are in mind who practise a gnostic kind of asceticism, believing (it seems) that matter and everything connected with it
3 (such as sexual relations) is intrinsically evil. *They forbid marriage*; so did the (later) gnostic heretics, e.g. Satornilus (Irenaeus, *Adv. Haer.* I. xxiv. 2), Marcion, and Apelles (Tertullian, *de Praescriptione* 33). Paul did not do this, though he scarcely shows the positive attitude to marriage and child-bearing found in the Pastorals (1 Cor. 7). It must be added that Paul's reservations with regard to marriage rested on grounds quite different from those of the gnostics. These also *inculcate abstinence from certain foods*; parallel prohibitions can be found elsewhere in the New Testament (Rom. 14:2 f.; 1 Cor. 8:7–13; 10:23–33; Col. 2:21b.) Such abstinence has not only a gnostic-dualistic background, but also a Jewish; food laws played an important part in the Old Testament and Judaism, and entered into the relations between Jewish and Gentile Christians (Acts 10:28; 11:3; 15:20, 29; 21:25; Gal. 2:12). The rejection of marriage is not answered in this context (though the author makes his view clear

though God created them to be enjoyed with thanksgiving
4 by believers who have inward knowledge of the truth. For
everything that God created is good, and nothing is to be
5 rejected when it is taken with thanksgiving, since it is hallowed by God's own word and by prayer.
6   By offering such advice as this to the brotherhood you will

---

enough elsewhere (1 Tim. 2:15; 3:2, 12; 5:9, 14; Tit. 1:6; 2:4));
abstinence from foods is rejected as contrary to the ordinance of God
in creation. It is indeed to the pure that all things are pure (Tit. 1:15);
it is Christians—*believers who have inward knowledge of the truth* (cp. 2:4)—
who may freely partake of all foods; they do so *with thanksgiving*—
that is, they say grace, giving thanks to God (after the Jewish model;
4 cp. also Rom. 14:6) over their meals. *Everything that God created is good*;
cp. Gen. 1:4, 10, 12, 18, 21, 25, 31. This is not in contradiction with
Rom. 8:20, 22, where it appears that the sub-human creation has
suffered some kind of fall parallel to the fall of man (cp. 1 John 5:19).
The Pastorals do not deny this, but do reject the gnostic view that
matter is evil in itself and from the beginning.
5   The precise meaning of *it is hallowed by God's own word and by prayer*
is not clear. 'Prayer' will refer to the thanksgiving of v. 4; but 'God's
own word' may be either the creating word by which material objects
were brought into being (Gen. 1:3, &c.; cp. also the repeated pro-
nouncement referred to above that created things are good), or the
true understanding of God and of his relation to creation which is
contained in his word (in the Old Testament).

3e. **4:6–16.** TIMOTHY'S CONDUCT IN FACE OF FALSE DOCTRINE.
The previous paragraph answered the threatening heresy on
first principles, by appealing to God's work in creation. But how
should a young minister behave when confronted by heresy in a
church for which he is responsible? What will *a good servant of
Christ Jesus* do in these circumstances to *further the salvation of*
himself *and* of his *hearers*?

In the first place, as a servant among brothers, not as lord over
6 subjects, he will hand on *to the brotherhood* at large the teaching he
receives from Paul. The word *servant* translates διάκονος, which at
3:8, 12 is rendered 'deacon'. Here, however, it clearly lacks the
technical sense which evidently was not inseparably connected with
it. The non-technical sense is much more common in the New Testament than the technical; cp. 1 Cor. 3:5; 2 Cor. 3:6; 6:4; 11:23;

prove a good servant of Christ Jesus, bred in the precepts of
our faith and of the sound instruction which you have fol-
7 lowed. Have nothing to do with those godless myths, fit only
for old women. Keep yourself in training for the practice of
8 religion. The training of the body does bring limited benefit,
but the benefits of religion are without limit, since it holds
9 promise not only for this life but for the life to come. Here
are words you may trust, words that merit full acceptance:

Eph. 3:7; 6:21; Col. 1:7, 23, 25; 4:7. 'Ministry' is a far larger term
than the particular forms that ministry may at any particular time
take. *The precepts of our faith and of the sound instruction* is a characteristic
expression. For 'precepts of our faith' (λόγοι τῆς πίστεως) cp. the
common 'Here are words you may trust' (πιστὸς ὁ λόγος). Faith is
often in the Pastorals connected with instruction (teaching). Timothy,
who is *bred in* the precepts and sound instruction, is a Christian of
the second generation; cp. 2 Tim. 1:5.

Over against the instruction Timothy must give to the Church
7 stand *those godless myths, fit only for old women*. They are not defined, but
presumably they at least include the subversive doctrines inspired
by devils (v. 1). For myths see note on 1:4. They may be full of the
word 'God', but they are godless, because they do not rest upon the
Christian revelation of God in Jesus Christ; they are fit only for old
women, because instead of encouraging that strenuous training in the
life of godliness which is called for in the following verses they pamper
human desires—not least when they take an ascetic form.

The Christian, and especially the Christian minister, must *keep
in training*; the metaphor is drawn from the games, a field of figurative
speech used by Paul, and by other moral teachers of the age. Bodily
8 exercise brings *limited benefit* (or possibly, 'temporary benefit'; this
rendering would be a suitable introduction to v. 8b, *not only for this
life but for the life to come*); but *religion*, and with it training for religion,
is a different matter (cp. 1 Cor. 9:24 f.). 'Religion' is a characteristic
word of the Pastorals; see note on 2:2. The language is not entirely
happy, since it might be taken to mean that to practise the proper
religious rites is sure to bring unlimited benefits here and hereafter;
but it is clear from the context that this is not intended. The Christian
religion means hope in God (v. 10), and arises solely out of his saving
work, not out of man's piety (cp. 1:15; 2 Tim. 1:9; Tit. 3:4 f.).

Life: see note on 1:16.
9 *Here are words you may trust* . . . See note on 1:15. Here it is uncertain

10 'With this before us we labour and struggle,[1] because[2] we have set our hope on the living God, who is the Saviour of all men'—the Saviour, above all, of believers.

11, 12   Pass on these orders and these teachings. Let no one slight

[1] *Some witnesses read* suffer reproach.   [2] *Or* since 'It holds promise . . . to come.' These are words . . . acceptance. For this is the aim of all our labour and struggle, since . . .

---

whether the words refer to v. 10 (as in the text), or to v. 8 (as in the margin). Neither alternative can be excluded as impossible, but the marginal reading may be preferred on the grounds (a) that v. 8, which resembles Stoic pronouncements on the relative worth of bodily and spiritual training, looks more like the kind of maxim cited in the Pastorals in this way than does v. 10, and (b) v. 10 is introduced by the word 'for' (γάρ, not represented in the present translation), which would not aptly follow the citation formula. In fact, v. 10

10 demonstrates the reason for the godly discipline: for *with this before us we labour and struggle* (these verbs take up again the image of the athlete; the former has sometimes the sense of *church* work, e.g. Rom. 16:12; 1 Cor. 15:10), *because we have set our hope*. . . . The present life and the life to come are both in the hands of the *living God*. Because he is living and the source of life he *is the Saviour* (see note on 1:1) *of all men*, whom he preserves in life, making the sun to shine and the rain to fall on good and bad alike. When 'Saviour' is taken in this sense it is possible to understand the last words of the verse: *above all, of believers*. God is indeed the Creator and Preserver of all mankind, but to those who put their trust in him the promise of eternal life is and will be realized, so that they achieve the eschatological salvation of Rom. 13:11. 'In a word, will [God] not, in every respect, keep them safe to the end?' (Calvin).

The variant 'suffer reproach' (ὀνειδιζόμεθα) is strongly supported by MS. evidence, but is less suited to the context than 'struggle' (ἀγωνιζόμεθα). If v. 10 is taken to be the 'faithful saying', this could be an argument in favour of the marginal reading; if, however, we are right in finding the 'faithful saying' in v. 8, 'struggle' may be preferred.

11   *Pass on these orders and these teachings* links vv. 6–10, which deal with Timothy's attitude to false doctrine, to vv. 12–16, which give him positive advice on the conduct of his own ministry.

12   The dramatic framework of the Pastorals is the giving of advice by an aged apostle (see especially 2 Tim. 4:6 ff.) to a *young* follower (cp. 5:1 f.; 2 Tim. 1:5; 2:1, 22; 3:10 f., 14 f.; Tit. 2:7, 15). The picture is not necessarily inconsistent with the facts, for Timothy

you because you are young, but make yourself an example to
believers in speech and behaviour, in love, fidelity, and
13 purity. Until I arrive devote your attention to the public
14 reading of the scriptures, to exhortation, and to teaching. Do
not neglect the spiritual endowment you possess, which was

---

was called into service at Acts 16:1, and if he was then no more than
twenty he would at Paul's death have been well under forty—young
enough for the responsible duties he was fulfilling. He was perhaps
an easily intimidated person (1 Cor. 16:10 f.). He had, however,
been for more than a decade a trusted lieutenant of Paul's, and this
verse, together with the reference to Timothy's 'progress' in v. 15,
cannot fail to suggest, though it does not prove, that we have here the
work of a pseudonymous writer, consciously but not quite successfully
reconstructing the relations between Paul and his young follower.
For the thought cp. Ignatius, *Magnesians*, iii. 1, 'You ought not to
presume upon the youth of your bishop'.

Timothy should be respected, not slighted; but a minister secures
respect not by the arbitrary use of authority but by becoming *an
example to believers in speech and behaviour, in love, fidelity, and purity.* As
always (cp. note on 3:2), it is upon the moral character of the ministry
that the author of the Pastorals insists most strongly.

13   *Until I arrive.* These words also suggest the dramatic framework
of the epistle. On the total situation implied see Introduction,
pp. 16 ff. The three activities here mentioned are all public (the one
Greek word ἀναγνώσει, 'reading', is rightly rendered *public reading of
the scriptures*). *Exhortation* (or preaching) can be distinguished from
teaching, though the two shade into each other. In these words (together with the prayers of 2:1–8) we have a picture of the church's
meeting for worship; it may be noted that there is no reference to the
eucharist. The due execution of these tasks depends not upon
14 Timothy's native ability but upon a divine gift, or *spiritual endowment*
which has been given him. This word (χάρισμα) occurs frequently in
Romans and 1 Corinthians for a spiritual gift enabling him on whom
it is bestowed to fulfil the tasks allotted to him in the Church; it is not,
however, as here (cp. 2 Tim. 1:6), connected with a special act or rite,
such as ordination. The Pastorals are not inconsistent with Paul's
teaching, though they probably mark a later stage of development.
It was *under the guidance of prophecy* (cp. 1:18) that Timothy was
selected for ordination (cp. Acts 13:1 ff.); that is, it had been ascer-
tained so far as was possible that it was God's will that Timothy
should be ordained to the work of ministry, and in the bestowal of

given you, under the guidance of prophecy, through the laying on of the hands of the elders as a body.[1]

15   Make these matters your business and your absorbing in-
16 terest, so that your progress may be plain to all. Persevere in
them, keeping close watch on yourself and your teaching; by

[1] *Or* through your ordination as an elder.

---

the endowment for this work God's will was the cause, *the laying on of
the hands of the elders as a body* being an accompanying act—not a means,
for *through* is a mistranslation ($\mu\epsilon\tau\acute{a}$ with the genitive must mean 'with',
not 'through'). In this phrase, 'of the elders as a body' represents one
Greek word (R.V., of the presbytery), here taken as a collective noun,
and a subjective genitive. In the marginal rendering (*your ordination
as an elder*) the genitive is taken as expressing intention or goal—laying
on of hands intended to make an elder, or intended to confer pres-
bytership; that is (in view of the Jewish parallel to be mentioned
below), simply ordination. The latter alternative should probably
be accepted (see D. Daube, *The New Testament and Rabbinic Judaism*
(1956), pp. 224–46; J. Jeremias, *Zeitschrift für die neutestamentliche
Wissenschaft*, xlviii (1957), 127–32; but the suggestion will be found
in Calvin's commentary) on two grounds. (1) It removes the contradiction between the present verse and 2 Tim. 1:6; this is not a
strong ground, for it would not be unreasonable on different occasions
to describe a joint act as 'the laying on of the elders' hands' and 'the
laying on of my hands'. (2) It recognizes a close parallel between the
New Testament expression and a regular Jewish phrase (s^emikath
z^eqenim, or s^emikuth z^eqenim) for ordination (that is, as an authorized
Rabbi). It should be clearly recognized here that parallelism of act
and phrase does not imply parallelism of intention and interpretation.
Timothy then was ordained an elder; we hear of no further ordination.

     The 'spiritual endowment' is in some sense potential, since Timothy
must *not neglect* it; cp. 2 Tim. 1:6, where the same thought is expressed positively. The gift must be employed.

15   *These matters* (and in v. 16 *them*) refers back to the whole of the
paragraph vv. 11–14, and perhaps further. For Timothy's *progress*
cp. v. 12. The word is appropriate to a young minister; whether it is
appropriate to Paul's assistant Timothy, at a time late in Paul's life,
is at least questionable.

16   Timothy must keep a *close watch on* himself *and* his *teaching*. The
author emphasizes once more the aspects of the ministry which are
most vital to him: the character of the minister, and the purity of his

doing so you will further the salvation of yourself and your
hearers.

5   Never be harsh with an elder; appeal to him as if he were
2   your father. Treat the younger men as brothers, the older
women as mothers, and the younger as your sisters, in all
purity.

---

teaching. It is doubtless true (see Introduction, pp. 17 f., 25 f., 32 ff.)
that he tends to write on a pedestrian level, but it would be in-
accurate and unjust not to observe the burning enthusiasm which he
inculcates and evidently shares. The work of ministry calls for the
dedication of every gift. *You will further the salvation of yourself and your
hearers* is a rather tame translation of 'you will save . . .', but it safeguards the fact (cp. on v. 8) that the author did not mean that the
ministry itself, however devoted, was actually the saving agent. God
only saves; yet his salvation may take effect through faithful preaching and teaching, and this is a truth no minister dare forget.

3f. **5:1, 2.** TIMOTHY'S RELATIONS WITH VARIOUS GROUPS IN THE
CHURCH. Cp. Tit. 2:1–10. Christian courtesy itself suggests
how a young minister should treat members of the Church.
Little comment is necessary. It is clear that *younger men, older
women*, and *younger* women are groups defined by age and sex;
this suggests that *an elder* (πρεσβύτερος) may refer not to an
ordained elder (cp. 4:14; 5:17, 19; Tit. 1:5) but simply to an
older male member of the congregation: '*Never be harsh with* a
senior man.' If this be so, it will follow that (like διάκονος) this
word was not, when 1 Timothy was written, exclusively technical; cp. 1 Pet. 5:1, 5.

3g. **5:3–16.** RULES FOR WIDOWS. At a later period in
Church history there appear traces of a regular order of widows,
who seem to have acted as female servants (deaconesses) of
Christ in the Church. It cannot be said that 1 Timothy refers
to such an order, though it is clear that a list of widows *in the
full sense* was kept. It was kept, however, for the charitable care
of these elderly and solitary women (vv. 5, 9); it was expected
that they should already as married women have performed
Christian service (v. 10), not that they should do so as enrolled

3   The status of widow is to be granted only to widows who
4 are such in the full sense. But if a widow has children or
grandchildren, then they should learn as their first duty to
show loyalty to the family and to repay what they owe to
5 their parents and grandparents; for this God approves. A
widow, however, in the full sense, one who is alone in the
world, has all her hope set on God, and regularly attends
6 the meetings for prayer and worship night and day. But a

---

widows in their old age. Unfortunately it does not seem possible
to trace a direct line of development in the position and service
of widows; it is, however, important to recall the care of Jewish
communities for such persons (cp. Acts 6:1).

3   The translation *The status of widow is to be granted only to* interprets the
Greek word τίμα ('honour') in the light of v. 9 (*put on the roll*, καταλε-
γέσθω). It is true that the word suggests more than respect; a cognate
noun (used at v. 17) may (but does not always) refer to an office to
which a man may be appointed, or to the remuneration he receives
for his office. But it is very doubtful whether so formal a rendering as
that in the text can be maintained. The Greek means: Honour, in a
fully practical way, by means of financial support as well as spiritual
respect, widows. . . .
    Widows who are such in the full sense finds its explanation in the rest
4 of the paragraph. There are two qualifications, (*a*) need, and (*b*) a
Christian record of service. Need should be met, if possible, within the
family. This not merely removes a burden from Church funds;
family loyalty is in itself something which *God approves*; cp. the fifth
commandment, Exod. 20:12. It is when there is no family, or a non-
5 Christian family unwilling to support the widow, that the widow *in
the full sense* appears, *one who is alone in the world*. In part, at least,
because she has no other hope, she *has all her hope set on God*, and practises her religion with uninterrupted assiduity. *Meetings for prayer and
worship* translates the same words as 'petitions, prayers' in 2:1; and
the use of the article (ταῖς) seems scarcely sufficient ground either for
introducing the word 'meetings', or for the use of 'worship' rather
than 'prayer' (προσευχή). Some at least of the prayers in which the
true widow constantly engages will be private prayers. She 'prays
continually', in the sense of 1 Thess. 5:17. The opposite of this kind
6 of widow is the one who is *given over to self-indulgence*. It is not licentious,
but luxurious, living that is meant; this kind of living is worthless, and

7 widow given over to self-indulgence is as good as dead. Add
these orders to the rest, so that the widows may be above
8 reproach. But if anyone does not make provision for his
relations, and especially for members of his own household,
he has denied the faith and is worse than an unbeliever.

9   A widow should not be put on the roll under sixty years of
10 age. She must have been faithful in marriage to one man, and
must produce evidence of good deeds performed, showing

---

she who lives it, though she supposes she is enjoying life, might as
well be dead, since she is of no use to anyone (*as good as dead*; literally,
'is dead while she lives').

7   Timothy must *add these orders to* those he has already been charged
to give in order that *widows*, like, for example, bishops (3:2), *may
be above reproach*. All members of the Church should be free of reproach,
but it is particularly important that this should be true of those who
hold public position within it, and draw their support from it.

8   This verse resumes the point of v. 4 (though it would be possible
to take the subject—τις—as any *widow*, that is, one entrusted by the
Church with the care of other widows). The man who does not care
for his own household (including widows who form part of it) *has
denied the faith*, because he has failed in love, and lacking love he is
nothing (1 Cor. 13:2); indeed, he *is worse than an unbeliever*, not so
much because many heathen and Jews did care for their parents as
because, having accepted the privileges of Christian discipleship, he
has refused its obligations.

       The author returns to his discussion of the qualifications of 'widows
9 in the full sense' (v. 5). It appears that a *roll* of widows was kept, and
thus that there was a fairly developed organization; there is, however,
no reason to doubt that the Church, following the Jewish model, did
organize its charitable relief at an early date; cp. Acts 6:1. *Sixty years*
was a good age in antiquity; the number of enrolled widows cannot
have been large, and most of the widows must have been too infirm
for active service to the Church. This point weighs against those who
think that in this verse the meaning of 'widow' (χήρα) changes (cp. the
different meanings of the word πρεσβύτερος; see note on v. 1), and
that the author is now speaking of an order of women church *workers*.
Faithful in marriage to one man: cp. 3:2. Good morals in a negative
sense are not a sufficient qualification. The widow must have en-
10 gaged in active good works. She must have *had the care of children*;
probably, but not necessarily, her own; cp. v. 14. Mental and spiritual

whether she has had the care of children, or given hospitality, or washed the feet of God's people, or supported
those in distress—in short, whether she has taken every
opportunity of doing good.

11　　Younger widows may not be placed on the roll. For when
their passions draw them away from Christ, they hanker after
12　marriage and stand condemned for breaking their troth with
13　him. Moreover, in going round from house to house they

---

care, as well as physical, is implied. *Given hospitality*; cp. 3:2, and note.
Washed the feet of God's people; cp. John 13:1–13; also Luke 7:44. It is
the reference to hospitality that suggests this practice, but the practice
itself suggests humility in service. The allusion here makes it very
probable that the author either had read John 13:14, or had heard
some oral tradition to the same effect. 'God's people' accurately
gives the sense of ἅγιοι, saints, not as morally perfect, but as members
of the holy people. *Every opportunity* generalizes the particular examples
that have already been given.

11　　Such women may be enrolled as 'widows'; but not *younger* women,
even though they have lost their husbands, *for when their passions draw
them away from Christ, they hanker after marriage.* The desire for marriage
in young widows is natural, and is not condemned: see v. 14. Celibacy
is asked of none, and is discouraged, save in those who, by reason of
12　age, could find it no strain. Women, however, will *stand condemned*,
not for marriage as such, or for second marriage, but *for breaking their
troth with* Christ. It is implied that a woman when enrolled as a widow
gave an undertaking—as it were, to Christ himself—not to marry,
but to engage herself wholly to the Church (cp. 1 Cor. 7:34). It is
possible, though less likely, that 'their troth' (literally, 'their first (or
former) faith'—Christ is not named, directly or through a pronoun,
in the Greek) means their original profession of Christianity; but it is
not easy to see how this is broken by a desire for marriage.

13　　*Moreover*: there is another reason why younger widows should not
be enrolled. The office of widow carries with it, in addition to
opportunities for service, temptations which they would find it difficult to withstand—indeed, it is clear that v. 13 was written not out of
conjecture but from experience. It is easy for a woman whose duties
involve a round of visiting to suppose that she is actively at work
when in fact she is only engaging in idle gossip, and it is hard for her
to avoid the danger of *speaking of things better left unspoken*. For younger
widows, there is a better way. They will avoid temptation and do

learn to be idle, and worse than idle, gossips and busybodies,
14 speaking of things better left unspoken. It is my wish, therefore, that young widows shall marry again, have children, and
preside over a home; then they will give no opponent
15 occasion for slander. For there have in fact been widows who
have taken the wrong turning and gone to the devil.

16   If a Christian man or woman has widows in the family,
he must support them himself;[1] the congregation must be

---

[1] *Some witnesses read* If a Christian woman has widows in her family, she must support them herself.

---

14   more good if they *marry again, have children, and preside over a home*. The wife and mother holds an office at least as honourable and fruitful as that of the enrolled pensioner and servant of the Church.

15   This verse takes up v. 13. There are opponents quick to slander the Church, and the moral failures alluded to in v. 13 give them their opportunity. It is freely admitted that their criticisms are not without foundation; some widows have *gone to the devil*; not for torment, but in order to become his servants.

16   The words *man or* are not well attested textually, but are generally accepted on the ground that a restriction of the principle of this verse to Christian women does not make sense; v. 4 makes it clear that children and grandchildren, without distinction of sex, are under obligation to care for their widowed mothers and grandmothers. This argument is not compelling. In any Christian household actual responsibility for the welfare of any widows it contained would be taken by the housewife. It thus follows that the marginal reading, which is well attested, may be correct. It is wrong to see in the *Christian woman* a widow (or other woman) charged by the Church with the care of a household consisting only of widows (cp. v. 8, and note); if this were so the *congregation* would not *be relieved* by her *of* its *burden*. For *those who are widows in the full sense of the term* see v. 3.

   The general drift of this paragraph is clear, though it might have been possible to improve the drafting of it. A society laying claim to philanthropic principles was under obligation to protect its weaker members, of whom none (in the ancient world) were more vulnerable than widows. If they could be otherwise cared for there was no need to burden the congregation, whose resources were doubtless small: if young enough, they should marry again, and thus come under the protection of a male head of a household; or their children or

relieved of the burden, so that it may be free to support those who are widows in the full sense of the term.

17   Elders who do well as leaders should be reckoned worthy of a double stipend, in particular those who labour at preach-

---

grandchildren might look after them. If these resorts failed, if the woman was elderly and left alone in the world, the congregation might step in, but only if satisfied that the widow would bring no discredit upon it. The widow must have a good record; must be a true believer; must not be likely to use the opportunities afforded by her privileged position for idleness and gossip. See Introduction, p. 32.

3h. **5:17–25.** CHURCH DISCIPLINE. This is a miscellaneous section. First comes a brief note on the status and reward of elders (vv. 17 f.). The special case of a charge against an elder (v. 19) leads to a more general statement on public discipline (vv. 20 ff.), which seems to be continued in vv. 24 f. V. 23 is not very closely connected with the context, but need not be suspected as an interpolation.

17   *Elders* ($\pi\rho\epsilon\sigma\beta\acute{\upsilon}\tau\epsilon\rho\sigma\iota$). The word occurred at v. 1, where it appears to mean 'older man', and not to bear a technical sense. It is found here, and at v. 19; elsewhere in the Pastorals only at Tit. 1:5. See Introduction, pp. 31 f. As early as Clement (*c.* A.D. 96) the elder had a recognized place in the order of the Church, and the beginnings of this development are to be seen in the New Testament (Acts 11:30; 14:23; &c.; James 5:14; 2 John 1; 3 John 1), though elders are not mentioned by Paul. It seems that in Tit. 1:5 the word has the technical sense (and does not merely mean 'older men'); but the present verse raises considerable difficulties. It would be possible to construct out of it four grades of elder: (1) elders; (2) elders who preside (lead); (3) elders who preside well (*do well as leaders*); (4) elders *who labour at preaching and teaching.* But this is far too complicated, especially since (if we accept the translation *stipend*; see below) a salary scale appears to be involved. The only satisfactory way out of the difficulty (see Jeremias ad loc., though the suggestions here differ in some respects from his) is to suppose that in this verse 'elders' has not fully reached its technical meaning but still means fundamentally 'older men', the sense of ministerial position being given by 'those who preside well' ($\sigma\acute{\iota} \kappa\alpha\lambda\hat{\omega}s \pi\rho\sigma\epsilon\sigma\tau\hat{\omega}\tau\epsilon s$; cp. Rom. 12:8; 1 Thess. 5:12). The meaning will thus be: 'The older men who are nobly taking on themselves the responsibility of leadership . . . especially those who. . . .' Many

18 ing and teaching. For Scripture says, 'A threshing ox shall
not be muzzled'; and besides, 'the workman earns his pay'.

---

ancient societies, including the synagogue, were governed in this
patriarchal way, and it is very probable that we may see here one
strand in the development of the Christian ministry. On the relation
between elder and bishop see note on Tit. 1:7.

Stipend. This word is the noun (τιμή) cognate with the verb (τιμᾶν)
used in v. 3 and commented on there. It should be understood in a
more complex way than 'stipend' suggests. Cp. 6:1, where the same
noun is, in a similar context, rendered 'respect'. The leaders referred
to are to be deemed worthy of greater honour, and of a larger
allowance. It is not clear to what the word *double* refers. There are
two possibilities. (1) All elders are worthy of respect and emolument;
those who do their work well are worthy of heightened respect and
increased emolument. If the arguments above about the meaning of
the word 'elder' are correct, this view, which is in any case unlikely
because it suggests the existence of so many ministerial orders, or
ranks, is impossible. (2) Good ministers are worthy of greater honour
and reward than widows (vv. 3–16). This is quite reasonable. The
widow is not a minister but a pensioner of the Church whose volun-
tary services will (it may be hoped) continue into her old age; the
elder, as *leader* (or president; it is important to note that this is a
different word from that rendered 'leader' at 3:2) occupies a more
honourable position. Further, he will normally (cp. 3:2) be a married
man, and in need of greater ('double') support.

Elders, it seems, fall into two classes: some, but not all, *labour* (on
this word see note on 4:10) *at preaching and teaching.* The whole body
of elders (themselves crystallizing out of the senior ranks of the
Church in general) constitutes the nucleus of leadership in the
Church; within this body some are distinguished by the special gifts
and grace which enable them to build up and instruct the whole
community through the word of God. Leadership, as distinct from
preaching and teaching, would probably consist in general direction
of the Church's affairs, the administration of discipline, pastoral oversight, and presidency at meetings and services, including presumably
the eucharist, though this is not mentioned.

Elders, or leaders, are to be supported by the Church. This is
18 confirmed by two quotations. '*A threshing ox shall not be muzzled*'
(Deut. 25:4) is used also in 1 Cor. 9:9 to similar effect. '*The workman
earns his pay*' may, as some suggest, be a popular proverb, but was
probably drawn, if not from a written gospel, from the tradition of
the words of Jesus; cp. Matt. 10:10; Luke 10:7. It is, however, noteworthy that the saying is not here ascribed to Jesus.

19   Do not entertain a charge against an elder unless it is
20   supported by two or three witnesses. Those who commit sins
21   you must expose publicly, to put fear into the others. Before
     God and Christ Jesus and the angels who are his chosen, I
     solemnly charge you, maintain these rules, and never pre-
22   judge the issue, but act with strict impartiality. Do not be
     over-hasty in laying on hands in ordination,[1] or you may
     find yourself responsible for other people's misdeeds; keep
     your own hands clean.

     [1] *Or* in restoring an offender by the laying on of hands.

---

19   The elder, who devotes his time and service to the Church, needs
       the protection which financial support can give. He also needs other
       kinds of protection. No man is so exposed to back-biting and reproach
       as the minister who discharges his office faithfully. It is important,
       therefore, that charges against him should be disregarded if there is
       any possibility of their having arisen out of personal spite. It is true
       (as Calvin points out) that the law involved (Deut. 17:6; Matt.
       18:16) is applicable not merely to elders but to all. Why then is it
       here applied specially to elders? It 'is a necessary remedy against the
       malice of men; for none are more liable to slanders and calumnies
       than godly teachers' (Calvin).
20   It is not clear whether this verse continues v. 19 or makes a new
       beginning. Does the author refer to sinful elders, or to sinners in
       general? The paragraphing of the translation suggests the former
       alternative, and this is more probable (see also below on v. 22);
       but the latter cannot be excluded as impossible. There is a presump-
       tion of the elder's innocence, and he must be protected against
       irresponsible charges; yet the possibility exists that an elder may sin,
       and his sin must not be hushed up, but rather *exposed publicly, to put
       fear into the others* (sc. the other elders—if this were not intended the
21   language would be strange). The solemn *charge* that follows (cp.
       2 Tim. 4:1) shows the earnestness of the author's feeling at this point;
       the purity of the ministry is of the deepest concern to him, and the
       way to preserve it is to *maintain these rules.*
           Timothy's duty is first stated in general terms. It is the duty of any
       judge, but especially of a Christian administrator, *never to pre-judge
       the issue*, always to *act with strict impartiality*. These injunctions to de-
22   liberateness in judgement (cp. *Pirqe Aboth* 1:1) are given a special
       application in the next verse, but unfortunately it is not clear what

23   Stop drinking nothing but water; take a little wine for your
digestion, for your frequent ailments.

24   While there are people whose offences are so obvious that
they run before them into court, there are others whose
25 offences have not yet overtaken them. Similarly, good deeds
are obvious, or even if they are not, they cannot be concealed
for ever.

---

the application is. The opening words are rendered literally: 'Do not
hastily lay hands on anyone.' But the imposition of hands was used
in more senses than one. The text of the translation takes it to refer
to (a) ordination, the margin to (b) the reconciliation of a penitent
offender. In favour of (b) it has been urged that the context deals not
with ordination but with discipline, and that ordination would be
carried out not by Timothy alone but with the assistance of the whole
body of elders (4:14). The latter argument, however, rests upon
what is probably a misinterpretation of 4:14 (see the note; to say
this is not to deny that the whole body of elders probably did take
part in ordination); and although the context deals with discipline
it deals especially (see vv. 19 f.) with the discipline of elders. Elsewhere in the Pastorals (1 Tim. 4:14; 2 Tim. 1:6) the laying on of
hands refers only to ordination and never to the act of reconciliation
(laying on of hands in reconciliation is nowhere mentioned in the
New Testament, unless here), and it will be best to take it in the former
sense. Hastily to ordain an elder who later would bring reproach
upon the Church and have to be publicly exposed (v. 20) would be
an act of shocking irresponsibility, and it would involve Timothy in
the sins of the unworthy ordinand (or, possibly, in those of the rash
men who in their 'folly and levity' (Calvin) urge him on to ordain).
At all costs, the responsible leader of the church must *keep* his *own
hands clean.*

23   But purity does not mean asceticism. V. 23 was probably written
with an ascetic kind of gnosticism in mind (see Introduction, p. 13;
this need not make the epistle very late—cp. Rom. 14:2, 21; Col.
2:21 f. See also note on 1 Tim. 4:3. It is part of the duty of a good
minister to take reasonable care of his health in order that he may
render effective service.

25   The theme of discipline is resumed, in more general terms, though
probably still in the context suggested by v. 22. The choice of ministers
requires no merely superficial scrutiny. Some candidates will be
immediately excluded by *obvious offences*; others, however, will make a

6   All who wear the yoke of slavery must count their own masters worthy of all respect, so that the name of God and
2 the Christian teaching are not brought into disrepute. If the masters are believers, the slaves must not respect them any less for being their Christian brothers. Quite the contrary; they must be all the better servants because those who receive the benefit of their service are one with them in faith and love.

---

fair show because their *offences have not yet overtaken them*. Like offences, *good deeds* also may be obvious; and the faithful pastor may be encouraged by the thought (and the encouragement is so strong that it upsets the balance of the sentence) that *they cannot be concealed for ever*. It is possible that these thoughts should be applied more widely; certainly they are true in a wider context; quick judgements of moral qualities are always unwise. But on the whole it seems probable that up to the end of the chapter (and beyond; see below) the author continues to think primarily about the ministry.

3*j*. **6:1, 2***a*. RULES FOR SLAVES. Notwithstanding the opening words of the English translation (*All who wear the yoke of slavery*) it seems probable that this short paragraph is addressed not to slaves in general (though it would not be inapplicable to any slave) but particularly to elders who are slaves. 'All who' renders ὅσοι, which could well mean, 'Such of the above as . . .'. For similar instructions to slaves cp. in the Pastorals, Tit. 2:9 f.; in the rest of the New Testament, Eph. 6:5–8; Col. 3:22–25; (1 Peter 2:18 ff.). Here two cases are distinguished: (*a*) that of heathen masters, (*b*) that of Christian masters.

1   (*a*) The decisive motive is missionary. If Christian slaves become rebellious *the name of God and the Christian teaching* will be *brought into disrepute* (whereas slaves should add lustre to the doctrine of God our Saviour; Tit. 2:10); the master will misunderstand the meaning of Christianity, and will never become a Christian. Slaves should rather count their (heathen) *masters worthy of all respect*. Note that the word here rendered 'respect' is that which at 5:17 was rendered 'stipend' (τιμή).

2   (*b*) Service to a heathen master might seem irksome, to a Christian master illogical. Within the Christian fellowship the master is a *brother*; why should the slave work for a brother? But this is a complete misunderstanding. You do not despise a man because he is your

3 This is what you are to teach and preach. If anyone is teaching otherwise, and will not give his mind to wholesome precepts—I mean those of our Lord Jesus Christ—and to good
4 religious teaching, I call him a pompous ignoramus. He is
morbidly keen on mere verbal questions and quibbles, which
give rise to jealousy, quarrelling, slander, base suspicions,
5 and endless wrangles: all typical of men who have let their

---

brother; you *respect* him the more, and give him the more gladly
the benefit of your *service*.

3k. **6:2b–10.** THE WAY OF ERROR. The Epistle begins now to
move to its close, with the present warning (which has a pendant
in vv. 17 ff.) and the exhortation and encouragement of vv. 11–
16 (briefly taken up again in vv. 20 f.). There is no doubt that
the picture of this paragraph was drawn from life; the danger
to the Church is readily comprehensible, and so, in face of it, is
the author's insistence upon solid Christian virtues and especially
upon a pure and faithful ministry.

2 *This is what you are to teach and preach* links the foregoing disciplinary
advice with the paragraph on false teachers. The peril of such teachers
3 is frequently mentioned in the Pastorals (see Introduction, p. 12; the
verb ἑτεροδιδασκαλεῖν (*is teaching otherwise*) is also used at 1:3), and
the word *wholesome* is also characteristic (see note on 1:10); correct
teaching is both sound in itself and health-giving. *Religious* (cp.
religion) too is a characteristic word (see note on 2:2, and in this
paragraph vv. 5 f.). Here sound teaching is further defined in terms
of the *precepts* (literally, words) *of our Lord Jesus Christ.* Some (e.g.
Schlatter) think that there is a reference here to a written gospel; this
is possible, but not certain. Cp. 5:18, and note. As elsewhere in the
Pastorals, the moral origins, accompaniments, and effects of the
erroneous teaching are emphasized. Its roots are in a false estimate of
the self. The heretical teacher thinks himself important and wise; he
4 is in truth *a pompous ignoramus.* He professes to be concerned with the
truth; in fact he is morbidly keen on mere verbal questions and
quibbles. This is not the way to reach truth, but to provoke *jealousy,
quarrelling, slander, base suspicions, and endless wrangles.* Nor are these
external consequences all. When men, under a hypocritical show of
profundity and esoteric knowledge, stir up strife by advertising themselves and departing from the essentials of the faith, they proclaim
5 to those who have ears to hear that they *have let their reasoning powers*

reasoning powers become atrophied and have lost grip of
6 the truth. They think religion should yield dividends; and of
course religion does yield high dividends, but only to the
7 man whose resources are within him. We brought nothing

---

become atrophied. They no longer have any means of perceiving the
truth (of the Christian faith). The fact is that they are treating *religion*,
of which they continue to use the phrases and the forms (cp. 2 Tim.
3:5), as a means of gain.
6   There is a sense in which *religion* truly is a means of gain—*does
yield high dividends*. This is to be understood in the sense of 4:8; religion
affords gain in respect both of this life and of the life to come. The
present verse contains another significant word (αὐτάρκεια), here paraphrased in the clause, *but only to the man whose resources are within him*. The
word was popular among the Stoics, with whom it was a commonplace
that, whatever a man's outward circumstances might be, contentment was itself great gain. If a man was content with his circumstances (cp. Phil. 4:11, where the cognate adjective is used), he was
wealthy. Another possible meaning of the word is 'sufficiency': religion coupled with sufficient resources is highly profitable. This,
however, seems remote from the author's intention. Nevertheless the
translation given here is not entirely satisfactory, and illustrates the
sort of misunderstanding to which the author of the Pastorals from
time to time exposes himself. To a Stoic, αὐτάρκεια did suggest a man
whose resources are *within him*; but, notwithstanding his use of Stoic
language, our author is thinking of a man whose resources are in
God. The context of Phil. 4:11 is instructive here. Like a Stoic, Paul
claims that he knows how to accept both abundance and humiliation
(4:12), but adds, 'I have strength for anything *through him who gives
me power*' (that is, Christ; 4:13).
7   That man has no resources in himself, and that the author in fact
meant to say this, is brought out in v. 7 ('un commentaire de
l'αὐτάρκεια'—Spicq), which echoes Job 1:21; Eccles. 5:15. This, the
general drift of the verse, is clear, but the construction is not. *Because*
might have been expected to introduce the first part of the verse, not
the second. (In Greek, the first part is in fact introduced by 'for' (γάρ,
left untranslated), the whole verse being explanatory of the preceding.)
There are several variant readings, and conjectures have been made,
but it is probably best to allow the text to stand. The final nakedness
of death demonstrates and underlines the initial nakedness of birth.
There was no point in bringing anything into the world with us,
because we shall not be able to take anything out. It follows that
between these two decisive moments of birth and death man should

into the world, because when we leave it we cannot take
8 anything with us either, but if we have food and covering we
9 may rest content. Those who want to be rich fall into temptations and snares and many foolish harmful desires which
10 plunge men into ruin and perdition. The love of money is
the root of all evil things, and there are some who in reaching
for it have wandered from the faith and spiked themselves on
many thorny griefs.

11   But you, man of God, must shun all this, and pursue justice,
12 piety, fidelity, love, fortitude, and gentleness. Run the great

---

8 ask for no more than *food and covering*. The material in vv. 7 f., like
10 the use of the word αὐτάρκεια, has many Stoic parallels; so have the
next two verses. The author, it seems, is careful not to condemn those
who are rich (v. 9), or riches (v. 10). It is the desire to become rich,
and the *love* of money, that lead not only to *temptations* and thus to
ruin and perdition, but also to much unhappiness—*many thorny griefs*.
The Stoic has his own reasons (and they are not to be despised) for
reaching these conclusions; our author, though he does not bring out
the point explicitly, assumes that men cannot love both riches and God
(cp. Matt. 6:24; Luke 16:13; James 4:4; 1 John 2:15), and that in
turning from God to riches they lose their true peace and blessedness.

3l. **6:11–16.** THE MAN OF GOD. Timothy *must shun all this—*
the attitudes and desires condemned in the preceding verses.
How he must conduct himself in God's sight is described
positively in this short paragraph.

11   Timothy, as a representative minister, and in contrast with those
who make wealth their aim, is addressed as *man of God*; the title
recalls the prophets in the Old Testament (cf., e.g., Deut. 33:1;
1 Sam. 9:6 ff.; 1 Kings 17:18; 2 Chron. 8:14) and means a man
upon whom God has laid hold for himself and for his service. Such
a man is both obliged and enabled to shun evil and *pursue* good. The
virtues Timothy must pursue are *justice*, *piety*, *fidelity*, *love*, *fortitude*,
and gentleness. These form a better aim than wealth. Justice (or perhaps
'righteousness', δικαιοσύνη) and piety are general terms; the next
three recall the 'faith, hope, love' of 1 Cor. 13:13 (cp. also Col 1:4 f.;
1 Thess. 1:3; 5:8); gentleness (cp. 2 Tim. 2:25) is a virtue specially
necessary in a teacher and leader.

12   *Run the great race of faith.* For the use of metaphors derived from the

race of faith and take hold of eternal life. For to this you were
called; and you confessed your faith nobly before many
13 witnesses. Now in the presence of God, who gives life to all
things, and of Jesus Christ, who himself made the same noble
confession and gave his testimony to it before Pontius Pilate,

---

games see note on 4:8. The words used here ($\dot{a}\gamma\acute{\omega}\nu$, $\dot{a}\gamma\omega\nu\acute{\iota}\zeta\epsilon\sigma\theta\alpha\iota$) refer
to any contest or struggle, not necessarily to a foot-race. 'Fight the
good fight' is not an incorrect translation. For the adjective ($\kappa\alpha\lambda\acute{o}s$)
cp. Thucydides VII. lxviii. 3 (where the same words occur, and Rex
Warner (*The Peloponnesian War*; Penguin Classics, 1954) happily
translates, 'We fight for something that is worth fighting for').
Timothy's vocation, as a Christian and a minister, involves hardship,
but it is worth while. By fulfilling it he may *take hold of eternal life*, here
thought of as a future reward which may nevertheless be seized by
faith now, not because Timothy is fighting a successful battle, but
because he has been *called* by God.

The meaning of the next clause is disputed. When and how did
Timothy *nobly confess* his *faith* (literally, 'confess the good confession')
before many witnesses? This sentence must be taken with the statement
13 in the next verse, that *Jesus Christ himself made the same noble confession
and gave his testimony to it before Pontius Pilate* (literally, 'testified before
Pontius Pilate the good confession'). The following suggestions have
been made (in addition to Commentaries, see E. Käsemann in
Neutestamentliche Studien für Rudolf Bultmann (1954), pp. 261–8): (*a*)
The reference is to baptism. Before Pilate (cp. Mark 15:2; John
18:37) Jesus implicitly confessed that he was Christ, the Lord. Similarly at baptism (cp. Rom. 10:9; 1 Cor. 12:3) Christians confessed,
Jesus is Lord. This was done *before many witnesses*, that is, in the
presence of the whole Church. There is much to be said for this interpretation, but it is objected that it does not take account of the paragraph, or indeed of the Epistle as a whole, which is directed to Timothy
not as a baptized Christian but as a minister. (*b*) Jesus was arraigned
before Pontius Pilate as a hostile judge, and there bore witness to the
truth (cp. John 18:37b). Analogous trials of Christians also took
place, and it is suggested that the reference is to an occasion when
Timothy made a good confession of faith when on trial before a
heathen judge. But it is objected that the author evidently has in
mind a single and unrepeatable act. (*c*) It is held that the occasion
of Timothy's confession was his ordination. For the many witnesses
cp. 2 Tim. 2:2. This view (it is argued) makes the best sense of *obey
your orders* (literally, 'Keep the commandment') in v. 14 (see the note)

14 I charge you to obey your orders irreproachably and without
15 fault until our Lord Jesus Christ appears. That appearance
God will bring to pass in his own good time—God who in
eternal felicity alone holds sway. He is King of kings and
16 Lord of lords; he alone possesses immortality, dwelling in unapproachable light. No man has ever seen or ever can see him.
To him be honour and might for ever! Amen.

---

as well as of the context. If an interpretation on these lines is accepted
it may be desirable to expand it as suggested by Calvin: 'By the word
confession I understand not that which is expressed in words, but rather
what is actually performed; and that not in a single instance merely,
but throughout his whole ministry.'

Timothy's work is to be done in the sight of God, the source of all
life, and of Jesus Christ whose profession before Pontius Pilate is the
basis of all Christian life and ministry (cp. Heb. 12:2), and in this

14 divine presence he is charged *to obey* his *orders irreproachably and without
fault*. A more literal rendering would be 'to keep the commandment
irreproachable and without fault'. This suggests an ordination charge
(possibly, however, a charge given to Christians at baptism) which
must be kept inviolate. The fight Timothy must fight, the charge he
must keep, have their term. The struggle lasts *until our Lord Jesus
Christ appears*. This thought will be both a warning and an encouragement to the minister. He will not despair, and he will not think of
himself more highly than he ought to think, if he keeps his thoughts
fixed upon the final victory of Christ. For 'appearance' (ἐπιφάνεια) in
this sense cp. 2 Thess. 2:8; also 2 Tim. 1:10; 4:1, 8; Tit. 2:13; the
word is often used of the glorious manifestation of divine persons,
such as (in popular thought) kings. The appearance is not necessarily

15 to take place soon. *God will bring* it *to pass in his own good time*; contrast
Rom. 13:12; 1 Cor. 15:51 f.; Phil. 4:5; 1 Thess. 4:15 ff.; Mark
13:30; where God's time is evidently believed to be near. But in all
these passages, as well as the present, it is God, God who alone is
God, beside whom there is no other, who determines times and
seasons (Acts 1:7). The author uses every means at his disposal to
emphasize the majesty and uniqueness of God. *He is King of kings and
Lord of lords*—this phrase differs slightly in Greek from that of Rev.
17:14; 19:16, and the difference emphasizes the fact that God is

16 actually the governor of all earthly princes. *He alone possesses immortality*. Men as such are not immortal; God in his mercy may raise
them from the dead and bestow on them eternal life, but he alone is

17   Instruct those who are rich in this world's goods not to be
proud, and not to fix their hopes on so uncertain a thing as
money, but upon God, who endows us richly with all things
18 to enjoy. Tell them to hoard a wealth of noble actions by
19 doing good, to be ready to give away and to share, and so
acquire a treasure which will form a good foundation for the
future. Thus they will grasp the life which is life indeed.

20   Timothy, keep safe that which has been entrusted to you.

---

in himself the spring of unending existence over which death has no
power. His dwelling-place is *unapproachable*, not because it is obscure
but because it is too bright for mortal eye. *No man has ever seen or ever
can see him.* The invisibility of God is a commonplace of Greek philosophical thought; the idea is paralleled in the Old Testament, though
the motive is different. In the Bible the fundamental point is not that
man cannot by his unaided reason discover the truth about God
(though this is true), but that man in his sinfulness cannot approach
the holiness of God; cp. Isa. 6:5; Rom. 3:19 f.; Heb. 12:14; &c.
    For the doxology cp. 1 Pet. 4:11; &c.

3m. **6:17–19.** TRUE AND FALSE WEALTH. The connexion is with
vv. 3–10, especially vv. 6–10. That which the world calls wealth
is a dangerous commodity; but there are better possessions.

17   The insecurity of wealth is a common theme in many literatures.
Those who are *rich in this world's goods* must not *be proud*. In view of the
vanity of human affairs (cp. v. 7) they should *fix their hopes* on no
human uncertainty (such as money) but only *upon God*.
    The author breaks off to make a characteristic point (cp. 4:3;
5:23). What he has said does not imply asceticism: God *endows us richly
with all things to enjoy*, and his gifts are not to be despised. Cp. Tit. 1:15.
18 But the best use of God's gifts is in *doing good*. To lay up treasures upon
earth is folly, since we can take nothing out of this world; *to give away*
19 *and to share* is to lay up in heaven *a treasure which will form a good foundation for the future* (cp. Matt. 6:19 ff.; Luke 12:33 f.), and to *grasp the
life which is life indeed* (cp. v. 12).

3n. **6:20, 21.** LAST WORDS TO TIMOTHY. In a last word the author
turns once more to Timothy himself (and through the figure of
Timothy to all Christian ministers).

20   *Keep safe that which has been entrusted to you.* The relative clause trans-

Turn a deaf ear to empty and worldly chatter, and the con-
21 tradictions of so-called 'knowledge', for many who lay claim
to it have shot far wide of the faith.

Grace be with you all!

---

lates one Greek noun (παραθήκη, 'deposit'). There is no question what
this word means: it denotes an object entrusted to a person for safe
keeping (in the Pastorals it is always used with the verb φυλάσσειν,
'to keep safe'; so here, and at 2 Tim. 1:12, 14). But what is the deposit
that Timothy must guard? It may refer (1) to Christian truth, whether
this be thought of as the fundamental truth entrusted to every Christian (and crystallized in the rule of faith, or creed), or as the body of
teaching which it is the duty of the minister to teach to others; or
(2) to a spiritual endowment, enabling the minister to do his work
(cp. 4:14; 2 Tim. 1:6). The former alternative seems more likely,
especially in view of the use of the cognate verb (παρατίθεσθαι) in 2
Tim. 2:2, and of the warning which follows in vv. 20b, 21. It is
worth noting (with von Campenhausen) that the Pastorals avoid the
ordinary word for tradition (παράδοσις), preferring instead the legal or
commercial word employed here. There is a difference between the
deposit of Christian truth and, for example, the 'tradition of men'
(Mark 7:8). Like Paul, the Pastorals emphasize the primary importance of the content of the Gospel. The Church's life depends upon the
purity and faithfulness of its doctrine. If sound Christian doctrine is
21 to be maintained, Timothy must avoid not only error but also *empty
and worldly chatter*. Plausible and impressive talk lacking substance,
and argument measured by sub-Christian standards, are a constant
temptation to the preacher and teacher. Of course, the sheer error of
those who *have shot far wide of the faith* is to be avoided also. *The contradictions* (ἀντιθέσεις) *of so-called 'knowledge'* (γνῶσις): it can hardly be
doubted that *gnosis* here refers to some kind of primitive Christian
gnosticism (see Introduction, pp. 13 f.). It has been suggested that
'contradictions' refers to a work under this title by the gnostic heretic
Marcion; this is unlikely, not only because it would make the Pastorals
impossibly late (it would be not impossible to regard 6:20 f. as a late
interpolation), but because the heresy combated in the Pastorals is
a *Jewish* gnosticism, whereas Marcion's was an *anti-Jewish* gnosticism
(Jeremias). The word may be a technical term in rhetoric, suggesting
clever but empty verbiage, or may simply describe the opposition of
heretics to the truth.

The entrusted 'deposit' has been set forth at large in the Epistle
(also in 2 Timothy and Titus, which may perhaps have been written
earlier than 1 Timothy—see Introduction, p. 19—not to mention the

Pauline letters, knowledge of which is assumed). It is contained in the 'wholesome doctrine' and the 'words you may trust' (faithful sayings): Christ Jesus came into the world to save sinners; was manifested in the body, vindicated in the Spirit, seen by angels, proclaimed among the nations, believed in throughout the world, glorified in high heaven; and so forth. The preservation of this Gospel message is Timothy's primary responsibility.

The Epistle ends, surprisingly, with a Pauline greeting (cp. Col. 4:18; 1 Thess. 5:28; 2 Thess. 3:18) expressed not in the singular (which would correspond to the address to Timothy) but in the plural: *Grace be with you all!* 'All' (not in the Greek) has doubtless been added in the translation to make clear that 'you' is plural. These Epistles were intended for a wide circle of readers, all of whom will need the divine grace if they are to fulfil their mission.

2 TIMOTHY

1 FROM Paul, apostle of Jesus Christ by the will of God, whose
2 promise of life is fulfilled in Christ Jesus, to Timothy his
dear son.

Grace, mercy, and peace to you from God the Father and
our Lord Jesus Christ.

3 I thank God—whom I, like my forefathers, worship with a
pure intention—when I mention you in my prayers; this I

---

1. 1:1, 2. THE ADDRESS

See the notes on 1 Tim. 1:1 f. Here only fresh points will be
noted.

1 *By the will of God* corresponds to 'by command of God' in 1 Tim. 1:1,
and is another way of expressing the divine origin of Paul's apostleship (cp. Gal. 1:1).

Whose promise of life is fulfilled in Christ Jesus paraphrases 'according
to the promise of life which is in Christ Jesus', and fails to bring out
the connexion between the promise of life and Paul's apostleship. It
is the life that is in Christ Jesus; it is true that God's promises are fulfilled in Christ, but this is not what is said here. The work of the
apostle is one means by which the life which is in Christ is to be dis-
seminated.

2 *His dear son*: cp. 'his true-born son' in 1 Tim. 1:2. Both adjectives
express, with different emphases, the close relation between writer and
recipient.

2. 1:3–5. THANKSGIVING

Very many Greek letters (including most of Paul's, but not
1 Timothy and Titus) continue with a thanksgiving immediately
after the address. The punctuation, but not the main intent, of
the paragraph is open to doubt.

3 The writer (in the person of Paul) claims that, *like his forefathers*,
he worships God *with a pure intention*. A more literal translation is,
'whom I serve (cp. Rom. 1:9; 12:1—more is intended than worship
in the ordinary, cultic, sense of the word) from my forefathers with a

4 do constantly night and day. And when I remember the tears
  you shed, I long to see you again to make my happiness
5 complete. I am reminded of the sincerity of your faith, a faith
  which was alive in Lois your grandmother and Eunice your
  mother before you, and which, I am confident, lives in you
  also.

---

pure conscience' (συνείδησις, translated 'conscience' at, e.g., 1 Tim·
1:5). The sense is the same as that of Acts 24:14 ('I worship the God
of our fathers'; cp. 26:6; 28:20): Paul has not invented a new-fangled
deity for himself. The God whom he serves in Jesus Christ is the God
of the Old Testament; there is complete continuity between the
Testaments (cp. 3:15). The reference to conscience is to be taken
closely with this assertion: Paul is entirely sincere in claiming that
Christianity is the fulfilment of Judaism.

Paul *constantly mentions* Timothy *in his prayers*; that is, whenever he
prays. It is possibly correct to connect *night and day* with 'constantly',
but equally possible (by a different punctuation) to connect it with
4 *I long to see you again*, and perhaps better, since the sentence as taken
in the translation is tautologous. Timothy *shed tears* at parting, and
to be reunited will *make* Paul's *happiness complete*. It is possible to re-
move the point between vv. 4 and 5 and to render, '. . . that my
5 happiness may be complete when I am reminded . . .'. Some think
that 'I am reminded' refers to news received from Timothy.

Like Paul, Timothy can look back upon predecessors in the faith,
though probably the reference here is to Christian forebears. According to Acts 16:1, Timothy was the son of a Christian Jewess, though
his father was a Gentile (and is not said to have become a Christian—
silence here probably means that he did not). Acts does not name
Timothy's *mother*, or mention his *grandmother*, and we have no other
authority for the names *Eunice* and *Lois*. It is, however, probable that
the Pastorals were written in circles in which traditions about, and
perhaps direct memory of, Timothy and Titus were current, and there
is no reason why the names should not be accepted. Timothy will
surely prove worthy of such ancestry. He is here referred to as a
young, unproved man; cp. 1 Tim. 4:12, and the notes.

Was alive; better perhaps, 'came to life', 'took up its dwelling'. The
Greek aorist might refer to the moment of conversion.

3. 1:6–18.

This is a miscellaneous section, the only unity in which is con-
tributed by the theme of the Gospel, the driving force behind

6   That is why I now remind you to stir into flame the gift of
God which is within you through the laying on of my hands.

7 For the spirit that God gave us is no craven spirit, but one

---

the author, as it was with the historical Paul. From this springs
Timothy's ministry, and Paul's, and the active confidence in
God, and the gifts of grace, by which the ministry is fulfilled.
Everything depends on men's faithfulness to the Gospel, and of
this their treatment of its preachers is an indication.

3a. **1:6–14.** THE POWER OF THE GOSPEL, AND RESPONSIBILITY
FOR IT. It is difficult to summarize this section under a title,
for the writer passes from Paul to Timothy, and from summaries
of the Gospel and its gifts to claims laid by the Gospel upon those
who believe, and especially upon ministers. It must be followed
from point to point.

6   *That is why*—because of the inheritance of faith into which Timothy
has entered. His privileges lay this obligation upon him. For the rest
of the verse cp. 1 Tim. 4:14; see the note. There is little difference
between the negative precept of that verse ('Do not neglect') and the
positive *stir into flame* of this. *Gift* here translates the same Greek word as
'spiritual endowment' there. If the marginal rendering in 1 Tim. 4:14
is accepted there is no contradiction between that verse and this in
regard to the persons said to have laid their hands on Timothy in
ordination. In 1 Timothy no one is specified; here it is the apostle.
Even if the rendering in the text at 1 Tim. 4:14 ('laying on of
the hands of the elders as a body') is preferred, there is no serious
difference, since *the laying on of my hands* does not exclude the participation of the elders.

It is not implied here (or in 1 Tim. 4:14) that Timothy had
neglected the gift of grace given him at his ordination, when God
granted him special equipment for the work of ministry to which he
was called. It is implied that the gift is not one that works simply
ex opere operato; it is received, as it were, potentially, and needs to be
put into operation by the faithful and believing service of him to whom
it is entrusted. *Through* is here a correct translation (of διά with the
genitive), as it is not at 1 Tim. 4:14. In view of the different preposition (μετά) there used it might be permissible to suggest that in the
present verse we have the διά of 'attendant circumstances'—imposition of hands was an attendant rather than a causative act.

7   Timothy may go boldly forward in the employment of his special
gift, for (and here the thought widens to take into account not only

8 to inspire strength, love, and self-discipline. So never be
ashamed of your testimony to our Lord, nor of me his prisoner,
but take your share of suffering for the sake of the Gospel, in
9 the strength that comes from God. It is he who brought us

---

ordained ministers but all Christians) cowardliness has nothing to
do with Christianity. For the form of the expression used cp. Rom.
8:15. *The Spirit that God gave us is . . . one to inspire strength.* Strength
(δύναμις) is in the New Testament frequently combined with Spirit
(e.g. Luke 4:14; Acts 1:8; 1 Thess. 1:5), and this reflects Old Testament usage, for there too the Spirit is the divine power operating in
the field of human affairs (e.g. Micah 3:8). One equipped with the
Spirit of power will be able to fulfil his vocation. To strength, the
author adds *love and self-discipline.* Christian strength, especially when
exercised by a Christian minister, is never arbitrary and tyrannical,
but always under control, and under the guidance of love.

8   With this power at his disposal Timothy should not be *ashamed of*
the Christian *testimony* he has to bear. Cp. Rom. 1:16; the parallelism is close, for not only are shame and power brought together,
your testimony to our Lord is the Gospel, which it is Timothy's duty, as it
was Paul's, to preach. Cp. also Mark 8:38; Luke 9:26; shame would
naturally arise in the proclamation of one who appeared to be no
better than a dead Jew.

Nor of me: men are often tempted to be ashamed of the Gospel by
reason of those into whose company it brings them—for example, o
Paul, *his prisoner* (cp. Eph. 3:1; 4:1; Philem. 1). Paul is Christ's
prisoner because he is in prison for Christ's sake. Timothy need not
be ashamed of his share of *suffering for the sake of the Gospel*; he may
rather gladly accept it since he faces it not alone but *in the strength that
comes from God.*

There follows, in vv. 9 f., a creed-like summary of the Gospel out
of which the divine strength flows. It is worth noting that it is not
introduced by the formula 'Here are words you may trust' (1 Tim.
1:15; &c.).

9   *Brought us salvation.* Though in the Pastorals words of this group
(σώζειν, σωτήρ, σωτηρία) are relatively more common than in the
genuine Pauline letters, they are used with less precision. In Paul,
salvation refers almost exclusively to a final eschatological act (cp.
in the Pastorals 2 Tim. 4:18); in the Pastorals (e.g. Tit. 3:5) it not
infrequently refers to a personal event in the life of the Christian. Here
it refers to God's redemptive act in Christ (cp. 1 Tim. 1:15), who in
the next verse is described as the Saviour. The personal application

salvation and called us to a dedicated life, not for any merit
of ours but of his own purpose and his own grace, which was
10 granted to us in Christ Jesus from all eternity, but has now at

---

of this universal act of redemption (cp. 1 Tim. 2:4, 6) is given in the
next clause: God *called us to a dedicated life*; literally, 'called us with a
holy calling'. The calling (a Pauline word; cp., e.g., Rom. 8:30) is
holy, both because it proceeds from the holy God, and also because
it calls to a holy life, that is, a life dedicated to God; though strictly
speaking the call is not to any kind of life, but simply to God (cp. the
Pauline κλητοὶ ἅγιοι, 1 Cor. 1:2; so Spicq). The hearing and accepting of this call is conversion (sealed in baptism, Tit. 3:5). Superficially,
this hearing and accepting might seem to constitute a human response
to the act of salvation; in fact, however, it is a process to which no
human works (*merit* is a somewhat inexact translation of ἔργα) contribute. Neither a virtuous life, nor an act of religious decision, form the
basis of God's call; he acts simply in accordance with *his own purpose*;
his purpose, however, is not arbitrary, but a gracious purpose (*his
own purpose and his own grace*; hendiadys). The Biblical doctrine of
predestination is brought out clearly in the next clause: God's electing
grace was *granted to us in Christ Jesus from all eternity*. There is no election independent of Christ, who himself *is* God's purpose. The new
(corporate) man in Christ is God's eternal intention, which is not to
be discovered by any kind of speculation but only in Jesus, in whom
his universal love is revealed.

This point the author develops next. The eternal and long-hidden
10 grace of God *has now at length been brought fully into view by the appearance
on earth of our Saviour Jesus Christ*. In 1 Tim. 6:14 the word 'appearance'
(ἐπιφάνεια) was used of the second coming of Christ; here it refers
to his incarnate life; 'on earth' is thus a legitimate explanation added
in the translation. The adverb 'fully' is, however, an unfortunate
importation (not made at 1 Tim. 3:16; Tit. 1:3, where the same
Greek verb, φανεροῦν, is used). The gracious purpose of God is *fully*
revealed not in the incarnation but in the consummating appearance
of Jesus Christ at the end (2:10; 4:8). For the word Saviour see note
on 1 Tim. 1:1. In the first Epistle it appears to be used only of God
the Father; here it is applied to Christ as the person by whom God's
saving purpose was put into effect.

This was done when *he* broke *the power of death and brought life and
immortality to light*, that is, in his own death and resurrection. 'Life'
and 'immortality' may be synonyms, but possibly 'life' refers to the
new life made available in this world, 'immortality' to its prolonga-
tion after death. The victory of Christ, and the bestowal of eternal

length been brought fully into view by the appearance on
earth of our Saviour Jesus Christ. For he has broken the
power of death and brought life and immortality to light
through the Gospel.

11   Of this Gospel I, by his appointment, am herald, apostle,
12   and teacher. That is the reason for my present plight; but

---

life, rest upon objective historical acts, but they become operative
through the Gospel (cp. Rom. 1:16—the Gospel *is* the power of God unto
salvation).

It is to be noted that most of the language of vv. 9 f. belongs to
contemporary Hellenistic religious vocabulary, which knew of the
formal and majestic *appearance* of divine kings who bore the title
Saviour, and of religions which offered illumination and immortal *life*.

11   The author (in the person of Paul) claims *by* divine *appointment* the
closest connexion with the Gospel (cp. 1 Tim. 3:16 and note), of
12   which he is *herald, apostle, and teacher*. By *reason* of his appointment
Paul has no human dignity but only suffering; yet he can obey his
own precept (v. 8), and is *not ashamed*, even in his *present plight*. His
confidence in God outweighs the pains of imprisonment and the
danger of death. His confidence lies (1) in the fact that he knows God—
the marginal rendering (*I know him whom I have trusted*) may perhaps
be preferred; and (2) in the power of God.

The word variously translated *what he has put into my charge* (text),
and *what I have put into his charge* (margin) is that which is used at
1 Tim. 6:20 ('that which has been entrusted to you', $\pi\alpha\rho\alpha\theta\dot{\eta}\kappa\eta$). It is
accompanied by the possessive pronoun in the first person singular,
and as it stands can mean 'my charge (to him)' or 'my charge (from
him)'. The same word is used again at v. 14 (nowhere else in the
New Testament), where it is rendered 'the treasure put into our
charge' (neither here nor at 1 Tim. 6:20 is there any possessive pronoun). In each of these three passages it is accompanied by the verb
'to guard' ($\phi\upsilon\lambda\dot{\alpha}\sigma\sigma\epsilon\iota\nu$; in 1 Tim. 6:20 and 2 Tim. 1:12 rendered
'keep safe', in 2 Tim. 1:14, 'guard'). In 1 Tim. 6:20 and 2 Tim. 1:14
Timothy must guard (keep safe); in 2 Tim. 1:12 the writer is confident that God will do so. If in 1:12 the 'deposit' is something Paul
has committed to God, we must think of his soul, or perhaps his
confident trust; God will not disappoint his trust, or permit him to
perish, even though in this world he must suffer. If the 'deposit' is
something God has committed to Paul, it must be *either* the divine
gift which was given to him (cp. 1 Tim. 4:14; 2 Tim. 1:6) for the
exercise of his ministry—this gift will never fail for God will guard it;

I am not ashamed of it, because I know who it is in whom[1]
I have trusted, and am confident of his power to keep safe
13 what he has put into my charge,[2] until the great Day. Keep
before you an outline of the sound teaching which[3] you
heard from me, living by the faith and love which are ours in
14 Christ Jesus. Guard the treasure put into our charge, with
the help of the Holy Spirit dwelling within us.

[1] *Or* I know the one whom . . .   [2] *Or* what I have put into his charge.
[3] *Or* Keep before you as a model of sound teaching that which . . .

---

or the truth of the Gospel committed to Paul to preach. This last
interpretation has the great advantage of giving to the word 'deposit'
the same meaning in all three passages, here and at 1 Tim. 6:20;
2 Tim. 1:14 (see the notes). God himself takes ultimate responsibility
for the Gospel he entrusts to his preachers; hence 'the word of God
is not shut up' (2 Tim. 2:9). On no other ground would the work of
preaching be for a moment endurable; whatever the failures and
sufferings of preachers, God himself watches over his word to perform
it. His care continues up to *the great Day*—of judgement and consum-
mation; cp. 1:18; 4:8.

This happy assurance the reader may share with the author; but
it lays an obligation upon him. Above all, it is Timothy's responsibility
13 to keep his teaching pure and sound. The construction of the opening
sentence in v. 13 is uncertain (see margin), and it would be possible
to repunctuate so as to detach the words *living by the faith and love
which are ours in Christ Jesus* from v. 13 and attach them to v. 14. The
marginal rendering of v. 13a is perhaps to be preferred. *Model*
($\dot{v}\pi o\tau \dot{v}\pi \omega \sigma\iota\varsigma$) stands first emphatically: if you want a model (of teaching), take that which consists in the words you heard from me. The
alternative translation in the text is possible, but in the context, in
which Timothy is urged to model himself according to Paul's example,
'model' is a better rendering than 'outline'. In v. 13b two additions
are made in the translation: *living* and *which are ours*. These imply that
faith and *love* are elements in the religious life. They denote the quality
of life Timothy must show as he teaches the truth he has received
(cp. 1 Tim. 4:12; 6:11; 2 Tim. 2:22; 3:10). It is possible that the
words refer to the content of the Gospel, *the sound teaching which you
heard from me*; but the parallels, and the repeated insistence of the
Pastorals upon the moral quality of the ministry, suggest that the
paraphrase is correct.

14   For *the treasure put into our charge* cp. v. 12, and 1 Tim. 6:20. It is not

15   As you know, everyone in the province of Asia deserted me,

---

clear why a different rendering of the word παραθήκη should be given
here. There are two possible interpretations: (a) the gift of grace given
to Timothy at his ordination for the exercise of his ministry; (b) the
truth of the Gospel committed to the preacher. The latter is preferable because (1) the idea of the spiritual gift is conveyed by the
next clause (*with the help of the Holy Spirit*); (2) almost immediately
afterwards (in 2:2) the verb cognate with παραθήκη is used for the
entrusting of doctrine by one to another; and (3) a different word
(χάρισμα, 1 Tim. 4:14; 2 Tim. 1:6) is used for the gift of grace. Thus
v. 14 follows closely upon v. 13. The primary duty of the minister
as he lives by faith and love is to maintain the purity of the apostolic
doctrine; or possibly, though less probably, is to maintain faith and
love as themes of the apostolic Gospel. In this task he has the assistance of the Holy Spirit; cp. v. 7. The Spirit is infrequently mentioned
in the Pastorals; see Introduction, pp. 23 f. When the Spirit is mentioned, however, it is not with any sense of strain or strangeness; this
was simply an aspect of Christian doctrine which the author saw no
particular reason to emphasize. It is noteworthy that when he does
mention the Holy Spirit it is as an agent who preserves the tradition;
cp. John 16:14 f. There is no reason for confining *within us* to the
ministry; the Holy Spirit dwells within all Christians, and thus lends
special aid to ministers in their special responsibilities.

3*b*. **1:15–18.** PERSONAL NEWS of the defection of some Christians, and of the faithful service of others. After vv. 1 f., vv. 16 ff.
form the first of the genuine Pauline notes incorporated (according to P. N. Harrison, p. 125) into 2 Timothy. On the question
of genuine Pauline fragments see Introduction, pp. 10 ff.
These verses are supposed to have formed part of Paul's last
letter, written on the eve, perhaps on the very day, of his martyrdom. V. 15 is excluded, presumably because it refers to an
event in Asia, not Rome.

15   It is not likely that this verse was invented by an editor in order to
add historical colour to his pseudonymous work. Phygelus and Hermogenes are not referred to elsewhere in the New Testament or in
early Christian literature. Cp., however, *Acts of Paul and Thecla* 1
(cp. 14), where Hermogenes the copper-smith is mentioned (with
Demas); also the *Apostolic History of Abdias* (M. R. James, *Apocryphal
New Testament*, p. 463). In the Ephesian riot described in Acts 19,
Paul was not deserted by all his friends: Gaius and Aristarchus were
arrested (19:29); the disciples prevented Paul's attempt to face the

16 including Phygelus and Hermogenes. But may the Lord's
mercy rest on the house of Onesiphorus! He has often relieved me in my troubles. He was not ashamed to visit a
17 prisoner, but took pains to search me out when he came to
18 Rome, and found me. I pray that the Lord may grant him to
find mercy from the Lord on the great Day. The many
services he rendered at Ephesus you know better than I
could tell you.

---

people (19:30); some of the Asiarchs were his friends and protected
him (19:31). There was, however, another 'trouble that came upon
us in the province of Asia' (2 Cor. 1:8; cp. perhaps 1 Cor. 15:32).
It is impossible to tell a connected story of Paul's ministry in Ephesus
and the province of Asia without the exercise of a good deal of conjecture, but it is certain that it was interrupted by serious troubles, and
nothing forbids the view that on some occasion Paul was deserted by
all his friends. Further than this we can scarcely go.

-18   *Onesiphorus* is mentioned again at 4:19; nowhere else in the New
Testament. In the *Acts of Paul and Thecla* Onesiphorus plays a favour-
able and fairly prominent part. In the *Acts of Peter and Andrew* he is
converted by the two apostles. All this material is historically worthless. It is suggested here that he was a native of Ephesus, where he
rendered Paul *many services*. It was when he *came to Rome*—possibly on
business, possibly as a Christian missionary—that *he took pains to
search me out . . . and found me*.

He was not ashamed of his master; cp. v. 8, also v. 12. In times of
persecution it was very natural to be ashamed of being connected
with an obscure and unpopular sect; cp. Mark 8:38. Onesiphorus was
presumably a man of some substance; here and at 4:19 he has a *house*
(household). Hence his ability to *relieve* Paul. The word may and
probably does cover both physical and spiritual relief; by ministering
as a Christian to his bodily needs Onesiphorus also refreshed and
cheered Paul inwardly (cp. Philem. 20).

Paul's prayer for Onesiphorus is that he and his house may find
mercy with God on 'that day', rightly explained as *the great Day* of
the final judgement (cp. v. 12). Onesiphorus's goodness, great as it
has been, in no way releases him from need of God's mercy; in this
only can he hope, and this Paul prays for him. Cp. Matt. 5:7.

That *the Lord may grant him to find mercy from the Lord* is a strained
expression, only a little eased if we suppose that one, but only one,
use of 'Lord' refers to the Lord Jesus Christ; but it safeguards the

2   Now therefore, my son, take strength from the grace of
2 God which is ours in Christ Jesus. You heard my teaching

---

truth that the ground of God's mercy lies within God himself. Neither
Onesiphorus nor Paul can evoke the mercy of God. God grants mercy
because he is merciful.

4. 2:1–4:5. CHARGE TO TIMOTHY

This paragraph contains various pieces of advice and exhortation, and covers a good deal of ground, which will be indicated
in detail below. The general context of the instruction is that
of Church life lived in the last age of history, between the resurrection of Jesus Christ (which is the starting-point of the Gospel—
2:8 f.) and the general resurrection, which has not yet taken
place (2:18). This accounts for the sense of urgency which
pervades the paragraph, the strict discipline which is expected,
and the prevalence of error and wickedness. In these circumstances it is above all imperative that Timothy should do the
work of an evangelist (4:5).

4a. 2:1–26. THE MINISTER IN THE CHURCH. As elsewhere in the
Pastorals, the charge to the minister spreads diffusely, and contains warnings for the wicked and instruction for the Church;
but the chapter as a whole is addressed to Timothy, and deals
with his relations with various kinds of person, and his behaviour
in various situations. It combines summaries of the Gospel with
summaries of the kind of response to the Gospel which may be expected in a man such as Timothy; but it does not integrate
Gospel and ethics as organically as does Paul himself.

1, 2   The first two verses take up 1:14, 1:15–18 being a digression. *Put...
into the charge of* represents the verb ($\pi\alpha\rho\alpha\tau\iota\theta\epsilon\sigma\theta\alpha\iota$, commit) cognate
with the noun ($\pi\alpha\rho\alpha\theta\eta\kappa\eta$) used in 1 Tim. 6:20; 2 Tim. 1:12, 14. Its
meaning is in accord with these verses. The truth of the Gospel has
been committed by Paul to Timothy; in the same way Timothy must
hand it on to others. The life of the Church is not bounded (as it
seemed to Paul—1 Cor. 15:51 f.; 1 Thess. 4:17) by a near *parousia*;
it will be necessary to transmit the truth to yet another generation.
It is by the divine word, the apostolic witness to Jesus Christ, that the
Church lives; hence the writer's care that the word should be guarded.
My son; cp. 1 Tim. 1:2.
Take strength from the grace of God which is ours in Christ Jesus. This

in the presence of many witnesses; put that teaching into the charge of men you can trust, such men as will be competent to teach others.

3 Take your share of hardship, like a good soldier of Christ
4 Jesus. A soldier on active service will not let himself be

---

expresses in more general terms the exhortation of 1 Tim. 4:14; 2 Tim. 1:6. It is of his grace (χάρις) that God gives a gracious gift (χάρισμα) to enable his ministers to do their work. Unaided, Timothy cannot fulfil his duties; the enabling gift is in no way merited.

You heard my teaching in the presence of many witnesses. Gnostic teachers (see Introduction, p. 13) laid claim to a *secret* tradition, from which they drew their doctrines; over against this, orthodox teachers stressed the fact that the Christian tradition was public; there were many witnesses who could verify that the apostolic doctrine had been maintained in the Church, so that the Church taught what the apostles had taught. 'In the presence of' is perhaps too precise a rendering of δ∟ά; it is probably intended to suggest witnesses attending at Timothy's ordination (or perhaps baptism). Spicq thinks of other witnesses, independent of Paul, such as Barnabas, Lois, and Eunice, *through* whom Timothy learnt Christian truth; it is perhaps better to think of the Church at large as attesting the truth of the apostolic Gospel (cp. John 21:24: 'We know that his testimony is true)'.

The previous truths of the Gospel must be committed to *men you can trust, such men as will be competent to teach others.* Note the two qualities sought: trustworthiness and ability to teach (cp. 1 Tim. 3:2; 5:17; 2 Tim. 2:24; Tit. 1:9).

The life of a minister, however, is not that of a respected school-
3 master. He must expect *hardship*, and endure it as a *good soldier*. The use of military language to describe the Christian and the Church was very widespread; see especially A. Harnack, *The Mission and Expansion of Christianity in the First Three Centuries* (1908), i. 414–18. In the New Testament see, for example, Eph. 6:13–17; 1 Thess. 5:8. Its meaning is evident; the writer 'means that all who serve Christ are warriors, and that this condition as warriors consists, not in inflicting evils, but rather in patience' (Calvin).

The author develops his theme in order to make a particular point.
4 *A soldier on active service* must attend to his soldiering; he will not please the *commanding officer* who enlisted him to fight under his standard if his attention is distracted to home and business. So it is with the soldier of Jesus Christ. It is true that every Christian must give undivided loyalty to Jesus Christ, but the context, especially the following verses,

involved in civilian affairs; he must be wholly at his com-
5 manding officer's disposal. Again, no athlete can win a prize
6 unless he has kept the rules. The farmer who gives his labour
7 has first claim on the crop. Reflect on what I say, for the
Lord will help you to full understanding.

8   Remember Jesus Christ, risen from the dead, born of

---

makes it clear that the author is referring primarily to ministers,
who should be set free from worldly business in order to give their
whole attention to their task.

Another popular saying (see note on 1 Tim. 6:12) is brought into use:
5 *No athlete can win a prize unless he has kept the rules*, either the rules of
the contest or the rules of training (these were not completely distinct
—for example, in the Olympic Games each competitor had to swear
on oath that he had qualified by training for ten months). We are
probably to think here of the professional athlete, and the point will
be that of v. 4—that full-time service and maintenance go together.
6 This is brought out in the next verse: *The farmer who gives his labour has
first claim on the crop.*

These verses are important because they bear witness to the development of a ministry which presumably was (unlike Paul's) a full-time
occupation, and was supported financially by the Church; cp. 1 Cor.
9:4–15.

The three metaphors, of the soldier, the athlete, and the farmer,
7 are in mind in the next verse. The author will not expound them in
detail; if Timothy will *reflect on* them he will see the point. But this
verse looks further back, to v. 3. The main point of this small paragraph (vv. 3–7) as a whole is to exhort Timothy to take his share of
hardship; and the metaphors, when duly pondered, suggest that beyond warfare is victory, beyond athletic effort a prize, and beyond
agricultural labour a crop. In the same way, Timothy's share of hardship will be followed by reward.

But that which makes sense of the minister's hard lot is ultimately
8 not reward but the Gospel with which he is entrusted. Timothy must
accordingly look beyond his present troubles and fix his eyes on
Jesus Christ. The words that follow are evidently intended as a summary of the Pauline Gospel as understood by the author. For *my
gospel* cp. Rom. 2:16; 16:25. The insistence upon the resurrection is
in truth thoroughly Pauline (cp. Rom. 10:9 and many other passages);
but the descent of Jesus from *David* is not characteristically Pauline
(see Rom. 1:3; 15:12 only). The combination of these two clauses,
even if not Pauline, is nevertheless not an inappropriate summary of

9 David's line. This is the theme of my gospel, in whose service
I am exposed to hardship, even to the point of being shut up
like a common criminal; but the word of God is not shut up.
10 And I endure it all for the sake of God's chosen ones, with
this end in view, that they too may attain the glorious and
eternal salvation which is in Christ Jesus.

---

the Gospel. *Born of David's line* suggests the fulfilment of Israelite
history and hope in a real human person, and *risen from the dead* the
eschatological irruption into this world (the world of David, and of
Jesus of Nazareth) of the supernatural and divine.

9   The Gospel which makes sense of the hardships its ministers must
endure is also their cause: *in whose service I am exposed to hardship*.
Like a common criminal may simply compare the fate of Paul with that
of the criminal; it may, but need not, mean that when the Epistle
was written Christians stood before the law as criminals. Cp. 1 Pet.
3:17; 4:15 f. This question bears on the date of the Epistle, but since
it is uncertain when Christianity was officially proscribed little could
be certainly deduced from a reference to such proscription here beyond the important fact that the Epistles could not have been written
by Paul.

Whatever be the fate of the missionaries, *the word of God* (the
Gospel message preached by the apostles and their helpers) *is not shut
up*. The word is what matters; the preachers and their fate are comparatively insignificant. God himself takes responsibility for the progress of the Gospel. Cp. 1:12, with the note.

10   *I endure it all . . . with this end in view*. 'With this end in view' could
be attached to the preceding sentence, with the meaning: The word of
God is not imprisoned on account of the fact that its preachers are
imprisoned. This would, however, give the words an unnatural
position, and the connexion of thought is rather: I am content with
my own fate because I know that whatever happens to me the Gospel
will continue; indeed, an apostle's sufferings can help on the work of
the Gospel (Phil. 1:12; cp. Col. 1:24), and Paul will gladly suffer
for the sake of God's chosen ones; literally, the elect (ones). Cp. Tit. 1:1;
also Rom. 8:33; Col. 3:12. God's intention for his elect is that they
should attain salvation and eternal glory in Christ. Salvation here,
as in the genuine Pauline letters, is something which men may hope
for but do not now possess. It is to be found in Christ only (cp. Acts
4:12), and its setting is the eternal glory of heaven.

11   Here are words you may trust:

'If we died with him, we shall live with him;
12   If we endure, we shall reign with him.
If we deny him, he will deny us.
13   If we are faithless, he keeps faith,
For he cannot deny himself.'

---

11   *Here are words you may trust* (cp. 1 Tim. 1:15). Some would attach these words to the preceding verse, but the balanced clauses of vv. 11 ff. suggest that they are the saying quoted, notwithstanding the initial 'for' (γάρ, untranslated).

     If we died with him, we shall live with him. The definite past tense (aorist, συναπεθάνομεν) suggests a definite past event—the Christian's conversion and baptism (cp. Rom. 6:3 f.; Col. 2:12); but the saying, or hymn, is doubtless quoted here because of the possibility of death in persecution; see below. The martyrdom of the Christian who has already died and been raised with Christ will issue in eternal life with Christ.

12   *If we endure*; again, persecution is in mind (cp. v. 9), though of course endurance can be spoken of in more general contexts (e.g. Rom. 8:25; 12:12). *We shall reign with him*, in the sense that we shall share his kingdom; cp. Matt. 13:43; 19:28.

     If we deny him; again, persecution is suggested. Cp. 1 Tim. 5:8, and especially the denials of Peter, Mark 14:30, 68, 70 ff. For the second part of the verse, *he will deny us*, see also Matt. 10:33 and parallels, on which it is probably based. The hymn has thus turned from comfort ('If we died . . . we shall live; if we endure . . . we shall reign . . .') to warning. In the next clause it turns back to the ultimate comfort of

13   the Christian soul: *If we are faithless, he keeps faith, for he cannot deny himself* (the last clause, which does not continue the rhythm of the couplets, may possibly be an explanatory supplement by the author, but the rhythmic scheme is not so rigid as to require this. Some think, but without good reason, that the saying originally ended, '. . . reign with him'). The only ground of security is not man's faithfulness but God's, that is, God's faithfulness to his word, to his promises, and to himself. Some interpret this clause differently, taking it as a direct continuation of the third line: if we are faithless, God keeps faith by denying us, and meting out to us the punishment that we deserve. But this interpretation is unsuitable to the context, and does not do justice to the Biblical conception of the faithfulness of God; cp. especially Rom. 3:2 f.; 1 John 1:9.

14   Go on reminding people of this, and adjure them before
     God to stop disputing about mere words; it does no good,
15   and is the ruin of those who listen. Try hard to show yourself
     worthy of God's approval, as a labourer who need not be
     ashamed, driving a straight furrow, in your proclamation of

---

14-26   From this summary of the Gospel in a trustworthy saying, the
        author proceeds once more to advise Timothy with regard to his
        personal conduct and the regulation of the community life.
14   *Go on reminding people of this*, literally, 'of these things'; that is, of
        the requirement that Christians should be faithful to Christ even at
        the cost of life, and of the promise that God keeps faith—though the
        connexion with the preceding paragraph is indeed not close. *Disputing
        about mere words* (λογομαχεῖν) was evidently not uncommon in the
        churches for which the Pastorals were written; cp. 1 Tim. 1:4, 7;
        6:20; 2 Tim. 2:16; 3:7; Tit. 3:9, and especially 1 Tim. 6:4, where
        the cognate noun (λογομαχία, 'verbal quibbles') is used. This kind of
        disputation is unlikely to achieve anything beyond the overthrow of
        the faith of those who listen. Those who engage in such wrangles do
        so with a view to gaining the approval of those who listen to them;
15   Timothy must rather try to win *God's approval*. He is a *labourer*, and
        God is the master whose adverse judgement would cause him shame.
        Driving a straight furrow, in your proclamation of the truth is a translation
        which accepts one possible meaning of the Greek ὀρθοτομοῦντα τὸν
        λόγον τῆς ἀληθείας. ὀρθοτομεῖν is a very rare word (here only in the
        New Testament). Literally it means 'to cut straight', 'to cut aright',
        it could therefore be applied to ploughing, but it could equally be
        applied to any other process which calls for straight or accurate cut-
        ting. It occurs elsewhere in the Greek Bible at Prov. 3:6; 11:5, where
        it is used (with ὁδός) of cutting a straight road. Another image that
        ὀρθοτομεῖν might evoke is that of the stone-mason, who cuts stones so
        that they may be built up together. The metaphor intended by the
        author himself must necessarily remain in doubt, but not his meaning.
        (1) Whatever kind of cutting may be in mind, in the compound
        ὀρθοτομεῖν, 'the stress is on ὀρθο-' (Lock); the word of God must be
        rightly handled. (2) There is in the context a contrast with those who
        merely dispute over words, without regard (it is implied) for the
        underlying truth. (3) God's workman must so deal with the word of
        truth that he may not be ashamed before his Master. The sense of the
        present passage recalls that of 2 Cor. 2:17, but there a completely
        different metaphor is used.

16 the truth. Avoid empty and worldly chatter; those who indulge in it will stray further and further into godless courses,
17 and the infection of their teaching will spread like a gangrene.
18 Such are Hymenaeus and Philetus; they have shot wide of
the truth in saying that our resurrection has already taken
19 place, and are upsetting people's faith. But God has laid a

---

16   A further contrast appears in the next verse. A man who is engaged
in handling rightly the word of truth must *avoid empty and worldly
chatter*. See 1 Tim. 6:20, and the note there. Such idle talk leads
further and further into godless courses—precisely this is its danger—and
17 will affect others also, *like a gangrene*.
18   *Hymenaeus and Philetus*; the former may probably be identified with
the Hymenaeus of 1 Tim. 1:20. These two *have shot wide of the truth*
(the same metaphor is used at 1 Tim. 6:21, and, differently translated, at 1 Tim. 1:6) and disturbed the faith of some Christians.
Their error is here stated, and the statement is a valuable comment
on other passages where error is simply described as 'godless myths'
and the like. They maintain that *our resurrection has already taken place*.
There is a sense in which this assertion is true; cp. Rom. 6:3 f.; Col.
2:12; 3:1. The heretics, however, must have intended by their proposition to exclude the notion of a future resurrection (cp. 1 Cor.
15:12). Their error amounts to a gnostic denial of eschatology which
so exalts the present status of Christians that it sees no need for hope
and faith. It probably included the belief that the existence of Christians was already immortal because divinized, doubtless through the
use of the sacraments.
    Small wonder that the faith of some is unsettled; yet there is no
19 need for fear. *God has laid a foundation* on which faith and the life of
the Church may rest securely. The foundation bears an *inscription*,
placed by the Architect and Proprietor of the building and indicating
his purpose and ownership, thus the 'notes' of the Church (Spicq).
The wording of the inscription is expressed in two Old Testament
quotations: *The Lord knows his own* (Num. 16:5), and *Everyone who
takes the Lord's name upon his lips must forsake wickedness* (Num. 16:26;
cp. Isa. 52:11; 26:13). It seems probable that (though the second
quotation is not exact) the story of Num. 16 is in mind throughout
(cp. 3:8, with its allusion to Exod. 7). Korah, Dathan, and Abiram,
who have set themselves up against Moses, are separated from faithful Israel and swallowed up alive into the pit. The application of this
narrative is clear. Hymenaeus, Philetus, and their company do not
belong to God's people (though probably they were would-be leaders

foundation, and it stands firm, with this inscription: 'The
Lord knows his own', and, 'Everyone who takes the Lord's
20 name upon his lips must forsake wickedness.' Now in any
great house there are not only utensils of gold and silver, but
also others of wood or earthenware; the former are valued,
21 the latter held cheap. To be among those which are valued
and dedicated, a thing of use to the Master of the house, a
man must cleanse himself from all those evil things;[1] then he
will be fit for any honourable purpose.

> [1] *Or* must separate himself from these persons.

---

in the Church). God himself knows what they are (cp. 1 Tim. 1:20);
and it is the duty of every faithful Christian to withdraw from their
company. God also knows those who truly are his, and in his knowledge of them (not in their *gnosis* about him) lies their hope.

21   The general drift of the next two verses is clear: the Christian
ideal is to be a servant fit in every way to do the Lord's will. But their
precise connexion with the context is not so clear. Presumably v. 20
continues the distinction which is made in v. 19. The Church contains
men like Hymenaeus and Philetus (v. 17); but they are not the Lord's
'own'. Those who truly are God's should separate themselves from
those who defile the Church. The co-existence of good and evil in the
Church should not be surprising; *In any great house* a great variety of
utensils is to be found, some *valued*, others *held cheap*. The difficulty
arises when, in the next verse, the metaphor shifts. In a house, utensils
made *of wood or earthenware* may well be *of use to the Master of the house*,
notwithstanding their cheap quality. The metaphor is applied in two
different directions at the same time, with consequent confusion.

There is a further source of confusion. The list, *gold, silver, wood,
earthenware* recalls 1 Cor. 3:12, on which it may well be dependent.
But the word *utensil* (σκεῦος) also suggests Rom. 9:21, which provides
the terms here translated *valued* and *held cheap* (εἰς τιμήν, εἰς ἀτιμίαν;
in Rom. 9:21, 'one to be treasured, the other for common use').
These words in the present passage must certainly be understood
metaphorically, and might well be rendered in such a way as to
bring out more plainly their fundamentally theological sense. The
'utensils' are intended for honour, or dishonour. The thought is, however, moving on a lower level than that of Rom. 9. That the author is
not referring, as Paul does, to God's predestination is shown by the
clause, *A man must cleanse himself from all those evil things* (there is much

22   Turn from the wayward impulses of youth, and pursue
      justice, integrity, love, and peace with all who invoke the
23 Lord in singleness of mind. Have nothing to do with foolish

---

to be said for the marginal alternative, which suits the context well:
'A man must separate himself from these persons'). The 'must', how-
ever, in both translations suggests an imperative which is not in the
Greek, which runs literally: 'If a man . . . he will be . . .'.

Fit for any honourable purpose (literally, 'for any good work') could
apply to a 'utensil', and so could *of use to the Master of the house*; but
dedicated (sanctified) shows that at the end of v. 21 the author is
thinking of persons. Metaphor is shifting to direct statement of truth.
One must expect the Church to be a mixed community (cp. Matt.
13:24–30, 37–43, 47–50); but faithful members of it can and must
separate themselves from the unworthy in order to be useful servants
of the Church's Lord. The Church which is founded on the Gospel
must practise godly discipline; see Introduction, pp. 29 f.

22–26   How is this to be done? Practical injunctions follow, addressed
primarily to Timothy, and through him to the ministry at large.
These take up again the paragraph which began at v. 14, and was
interrupted by the reference to Hymenaeus, Philetus, and their like.

22   For this verse see 1 Tim. 6:11. *The wayward impulses of youth* may
be explained by the 'many foolish harmful desires' of 1 Tim. 6:9
(where 'desires' = ἐπιθυμίαι = 'wayward impulses' in the present
verse). The translation here, which need not suggest more than boyish
fancies, is scarcely strong enough. *Justice, integrity* (= πίστις =
'fidelity' in 1 Tim. 6:11), *love* are all in 1 Tim. 6:11: see the note.
Peace is added here, because the peace of the Church is threatened
by those who teach false doctrine (e.g. vv. 16 ff., 23). *All who invoke
the Lord in singleness of mind* means 'all sincere Christians', in contrast
with those who use the Christian profession as a means of securing an
audience for heretical doctrines. A Christian must never cease to *love*,
but it is not his duty to seek *peace* with those who twist the Gospel. 'In
singleness of mind' (literally 'from a pure heart') recalls 1 Tim. 1:5,
where, however, the translation of the same Greek is quite different.

23   For this verse cp. 1 Tim. 4:7; 6:4, 20. Timothy must tread the
narrow path between acquiescence in error, and too violent a rejection of it; his aim must be not to defeat his opponents but to win them
to a better mind. He should therefore not take part in *foolish and
ignorant speculations* (or, perhaps, 'debates'); in some circumstances it is
possible for the orthodox to become as foolish as their opponents. And
arguments *breed quarrels*, in which personal animosity drives out any

and ignorant speculations. You know they breed quarrels,
24 and the servant of the Lord must not be quarrelsome, but
kindly towards all. He should be a good teacher, tolerant,
25 and gentle when discipline is needed for the refractory. The
Lord may grant them a change of heart and show them the
26 truth, and thus they may come to their senses and escape
from the devil's snare, in which they have been caught and
held at his will.[1]

[1] *Or* escape from the devil's snare, caught now by God and made subject
to his will.

4f. desire to find the truth. *The servant of the Lord*, who must fight the good
fight of faith (1 Tim. 6:12), must *not be quarrelsome* (μάχεσθαι). The
virtues required of him here are similar to those mentioned in 1 Tim.
3:2 ff.; Tit. 1:7. For example, *kindly, tolerant, gentle* recall the 'forbearing disposition' of 1 Tim. 3:3, though different words are used.
He must be *a good teacher*, and must instruct and discipline *the refractory*. The disputes he must avoid (v. 23) are uninstructed (ἀπαιδεύ-
τους); instead he must instruct, or *discipline* (παιδεύειν) those who
would dispute. The aim of his instruction is expressed in v. 25b. Those
who are in error will not reach the truth simply by study and teaching. The teacher's work becomes effective only if God grants *them
a change of heart*. 'Our labours and exertions are thus of no advantage
in themselves; and yet, through the grace of God, they are not fruitless' (Calvin; cp. 1 Cor. 3:6). The paraphrase *show them the truth*
conceals an expression (ἐπίγνωσις ἀληθείας) characteristic of the
Pastorals: 1 Tim. 2:4 (come to know the truth); 2 Tim. 3:7 (a knowledge of the truth); Tit. 1:1 (knowledge of the truth). Here, and
probably elsewhere, it has an anti-gnostic ring. There are men who
profess to have knowledge (*gnosis*) of the truth; it is to be hoped that
they may repent and so gain real knowledge (*epi-gnosis*).

26 The misfortune of these men is not merely ignorance; or rather,
this is an inadequate way of describing it. They are in *the devil's snare*;
cp. 1 Tim. 3:7. From this, repentance and knowledge of the truth
(the author's anti-gnostic polemic does not enable him to escape this
statement; the crux of the gnostic problem was that Christians were
obliged to use language similar to that of the gnostics, however
different their meaning) will enable them to *escape*.

The second part of this verse is ambiguous (as the marginal rendering shows), because the author uses pronouns which might apply
either to God (v. 25) or to the devil (v. 26). The clause may refer to

3   You must face the fact: the final age of this world is to be a
2   time of troubles. Men will love nothing but money and self;

---

the devil's capture, or to God's releasing men from the devil that they
may thereby enter into his service. The verb used (*caught*, ζωγρεῖν)
means 'to capture alive', and since we hear of the devil's trap it is
very probable that it is the devil who is here thought of as capturing
men. *He* captures men, and forces them to do *his* will. This interpretation makes the easiest sense, but it does some violence to the
pronouns, and it is possible that the last words (εἰς τὸ ἐκείνου θέλημα)
refer back to God, and are connected grammatically with ἀνανήψωσιν
('come to their senses'); the purpose of deliverance is the doing of
God's will. The sentence could thus be rendered: '. . . escape from the
devil's snare (in which they have been caught by him—the devil),
in order to do his (God's) will.'

4b. **3:1-17.** TROUBLES OF THE LAST TIMES, AND HOW TIMOTHY
MUST MEET THEM. It is only to be expected that wickedness
should increase, and the troubles of Christians grow more
severe. It seems clear that the author is describing things as he
knew them in his own day—the future to Paul, but the present
to himself. In vv. 1–9 we hear of the wickedness of men, including some at least who are ostensible Christians. In vv. 10 ff.
Paul's own sufferings are recalled. V. 13 returns to the wicked,
and vv. 14–17 to the man of God and his equipment, with
special reference to scripture.

1   *The final age of this world is to be a time of troubles.* The time of affliction
    expected before the end of history is a commonplace in the apoca-
    lypses; here the notion (often conceived in supernatural or political
    terms) is strongly moralized. It is an important truth that the Church
    still lives in this 'final age' of trouble and distress, though true also
    that the author of the Pastorals probably thought that this final age
    would be chronologically much shorter than it has proved to be.

2   *Men will love nothing but money and self*: the paraphrase reverses the
    order of the Greek, in which all-embracing self-love precedes the love
    of money, which is a particular form that self-love may take. Cp.
    v. 4 (literally, 'lovers of pleasure rather than lovers of God').
        Arrogant, boastful, and abusive. The first two adjectives between them
    give the sense of ἀλαζόνες, ὑπερήφανοι, though the ἀλαζών is a boastful
    fraud, perhaps, rather than a really arrogant man. 'Abusive' (βλάσ-
    φημοι) might be 'blasphemers' (i.e. abusive of God); cp. 1 Tim. 1:13;
    also 6:1.

they will be arrogant, boastful, and abusive; with no respect
3 for parents, no gratitude, no piety, no natural affection; they
will be implacable in their hatreds, scandal-mongers, in-
4 temperate and fierce, strangers to all goodness, traitors, adven-
turers, swollen with self-importance. They will be men who
5 put pleasure in the place of God, men who preserve the outward form of religion, but are a standing denial of its reality.
6 Keep clear of men like these. They are the sort that insinuate
themselves into private houses and there get miserable women
into their clutches, women burdened with a sinful past, and
7 led on by all kinds of desires, who are always wanting to be
taught, but are incapable of reaching a knowledge of the
8 truth. As Jannes and Jambres defied Moses, so these men

---

4   The list as a whole resembles other New Testament lists of vices
in several respects; cp. Rom. 1:29–32. Its components are too clear
to require explanation, but together they constitute a shocking picture of Church life—of Church life, for it is part of the indictment that
the sinners maintain a religious profession and in fact pass themselves
5   off as Christian propagandists. Cp. v. 2. *Religion* is a common word in
the Pastorals; see note on 1 Tim 2:2. This verse indicates well the
twofold meaning which the word has in the Pastorals. It includes an
outward form, which may be hypocritically assumed, though it is not
for this reason bad in itself; it has also an inward force ($\delta\acute{v}\nu\alpha\mu\iota s$,
reality), which may be lost even when the outward form is *preserved*.
Keep clear of men like these. The translation does not render $\kappa\alpha\acute{\iota}$ (these
also); cp. 2:16, 23.
5 f.   A particular example follows. There are some—Christians, presumably, perhaps ministers—who take advantage of the weakness of
others. They *insinuate themselves into private houses and there get into their
clutches miserable women* ($\gamma\nu\nu\alpha\iota\kappa\acute{\alpha}\rho\iota\alpha$; 'silly' might be a better adjective
than 'miserable'). These women are aware of what is doubtless a
genuine need (*burdened with a sinful past*), but under the guidance
which is thrust upon them they have no chance of truly satisfying it.
A knowledge of the truth translates the phrase which occurs at 2:25; the
true servant of God may bring men to this, but not the counterfeit.
Only true knowledge of God in Jesus Christ can deal effectively with
sins.
8 f.   There is a precedent for such men and their folly. *Jannes and
Jambres* were (according to Jewish traditions propagated also in

defy the truth; they have lost the power to reason, and they
9 cannot pass the tests of faith. But their successes will be
short-lived, for, like those opponents of Moses, they will
come to be recognized by everyone for the fools they are.

10   But you, my son, have followed, step by step, my teaching
and my manner of life, my resolution, my faith, patience, and
11 spirit of love, and my fortitude under persecutions and suf-

---

early Christian circles) magicians who *defied Moses* before Pharaoh
(Exod. 7:11, 22; for many quotations see Dibelius–Conzelmann).
Similarly (the parallel is not pressed in allegorical or typological
detail) the heretics of the present day *defy the truth*. As often, it is
emphasized that these men who lay stress on their knowledge (*gnosis*)
are in fact foolish: *they have lost the power to reason*—a free translation
of 'men who are corrupt in mind' (cp. 1 Tim. 4:2 and note). This
description recalls Rom. 1:28, as does the next clause (*they cannot pass
the tests of faith*), which contains the word ἀδόκιμος (rendered 'de-
praved' in Rom. 1:28). This word conveys the sense not so much of
failure in an examination as of divine reprobation. The reference to
the past (Jannes and Jambres) brings encouragement for the future.
Their successes will be short-lived, for their folly will be as easily exposed
as that of Jannes and Jambres (there is probably an allusion here to a
lost tradition in which the two Egyptian magicians were shown up as
fools).

10   *But you, my son*. The last two words have no equivalent in the Greek;
they are perhaps intended to bring out the fact that the pronoun is
emphatic: *You*, in contrast with those mentioned in the preceding
verses. You *have followed, step by step* translates one word παρηκολούθησας
(or possibly the variant παρηκολούθηκας, perfect). It is a verb difficult
to render in view of the different words (*teaching*, &c.) which follow
in the dative—a difficulty reflected in the paraphrase. The meaning
is that Timothy has accompanied and observed, and also in a measure
participated in, the activities, events, and attitudes mentioned.
Teaching, in this context, is not only 'what I teach' but 'the way I
11 teach'. *Faith* should perhaps be 'fidelity' (as at 1 Tim. 4:12). *My
fortitude under persecutions and sufferings*: literally, 'fortitude, persecutions, sufferings'; see note above on 'followed'. Timothy has in fact
'followed' (in the sense given above) both the fortitude, and the
persecutions and sufferings.
    Antioch: see Acts 13:14–52; 14:21 (the context shows that Pisidian
Antioch is meant); *Iconium*: see Acts 14:1–5, 21; *Lystra*: see Acts

ferings—all that I went through at Antioch, at Iconium, at
Lystra, all the persecutions I endured; and the Lord rescued
12 me out of them all. Yes, persecution will come to all who want
13 to live a godly life as Christians, whereas wicked men and
charlatans will make progress from bad to worse, deceiving and
14 deceived. But for your part, stand by the truths you have
learned and are assured of. Remember from whom you learned

14:6–20, 21. It was in this region that Timothy joined Paul, though
not until a later point in the narrative of Acts (16:1–3, Lystra and
Iconium). If these verses were not written by Paul they may be held
to show knowledge of Acts—possibly the earliest known evidence
of its existence. Alternatively, they may reflect traditions about,
perhaps emanating from, Timothy.

The Lord rescued me out of them all. For the deliverance of Paul from
his persecutions see the passages in Acts mentioned above.

12 Persecution is not the lot of Paul only. *All who want to live a godly
life as Christians* (ζῆν εὐσεβῶς ἐν Χριστῷ Ἰησοῦ; cp. Tit. 2:12) may expect persecution. Cp. 2:3; the enduring of hardship is especially the
lot of ministers, but it is to be expected by all who take on themselves
the sign of the Cross. They will suffer, as others pursue their evil
13 courses. *Charlatans* (γόητες) probably looks back to Jannes and Jambres, and their like. Such men are both *deceiving and deceived* (sc. by
the devil, and by other charlatans). This expression seems to have
been current, and in this connexion cp. Philo, *de Mig. Abr.* 83:
'. . . Those who use charms and enchantments [Philo refers to Exod.
7] . . . they are cheated . . . while they think that they are cheating.'

Will make progress: προκόψουσιν. The same word occurs in v. 9, with
the negative (paraphrased as, 'their successes will be short-lived').
The observation that v. 13 declares that the deceivers will go from
bad to worse, whereas v. 9 denies that they will meet with permanent
success, only partially removes the apparent contradiction.

14 In this verse the author turns back to Timothy with the same words
that he used in v. 10. *Remember* adds a second imperative, whereas the
Greek (εἰδώς, 'knowing'—participle) gives the reasons why Timothy
should *stand by the truths* he has *learned and* is *assured of*. The reasons are
two. (1) He knows *from whom* (the English pronoun could be singular
or plural; the Greek text is uncertain, but it is probably correct to read
the plural form of the pronoun, though the singular—referring simply
to Paul—is well attested) he *learned them*. (2) He has long been
familiar with scripture, on which they are based. The Pastorals lay

15 them; remember that from early childhood you have been
familiar with the sacred writings which have power to make
you wise and lead you to salvation through faith in Christ
16 Jesus. Every inspired scripture has its use for teaching the

some stress on the personal relations through which the Christian
tradition is handed down. Paul knows Timothy to be a trustworthy
person, and Timothy that he can accept Paul's teaching (e.g. vv. 10f.);
Timothy in turn must commit the truth to trustworthy men who again
will hand it on (2:2). Personal acquaintance is essential in the process, and it is the truth of the Gospel that is transmitted, by teaching
and learning. No formal succession of ministers is in mind: Timothy's
mother and grandmother are important links in the chain (1:5).
The Christian truth in which Timothy has been orally instructed is
supported by the familiarity he has had *from early childhood* (cp. 1:5;
Acts 16:1) *with the sacred writings*. These are undoubtedly the Old
Testament; the expression was common in Hellenistic Judaism.
Together with the Christian tradition transmitted orally they constitute a close equivalent to the Christian Bible, which is the foundation of the Christian ministry. The sacred writings *have power to make
you wise and lead you to salvation*. The end of the true wisdom imparted
by scripture is salvation. The Old Testament itself is a book of salvation, narrating the mighty deeds of God in delivering his people in
old time, and also pointing forward to his final saving act in Christ.
The law, though not as such applicable to Christians (1 Tim. 1:9), is
itself part of the saving activity of God. It can be seen in this light,
however, only *through faith in Christ Jesus*. This phrase is not a mere
pendant, added almost absent-mindedly (as has been suggested)
after the word salvation. The salvation to which the Old Testament
points is not independent of Christ. This must be borne in mind in
reading the next two verses, which develop further the importance
and use of scripture.

16   *Every inspired scripture has its use.* . . . An alternative translation would
be, 'All scripture is inspired and has its use . . .'. The alternative has
the advantage that it translates the word καί (and, also). But the rendering in the text (or better, '. . . *also* (καί) has its use . . .') is to be
preferred, for scripture in Greek (γραφή, literally 'writing') needs an
adjective. It would be absurd to say, 'Every writing is inspired'.
Where inspiration does exist it may spring from various sources, and
the Greek word (θεόπνευστος) makes it clear that the inspiration of
Holy Scripture, and thus Holy Scripture itself, is from God. No
attempt is made here to answer the more complicated but less important question, through what human channels the divine inspiration
flowed. Scripture is useful (1) in the field of doctrine, both positively

truth and refuting error, or for reformation of manners and
17 discipline in right living, so that the man who belongs to
God may be efficient and equipped for good work of every
kind.

4   Before God, and before Christ Jesus who is to judge men

---

and negatively; (2) in the field of ethics. It is interesting to note a
close parallel to the words of this verse in Epictetus (III. xxi. 15): 'In
this way the mysteries are useful (ὠφέλιμα); in this way we come to
the notion that all these things were established by the ancients for
the discipline and correction of life (ἐπὶ παιδείᾳ καὶ ἐπανορθώσει τοῦ
βίου).' Even when the thought of the Pastorals is most Biblical the
author can show contacts with the literature of contemporary moral
philosophy.

17   *The man who belongs to God*: cp. 1 Tim. 6:11. The phrase could
simply refer to the Christian, who certainly belongs to God; the
context, however, suggests a special reference to the minister. It is
he primarily who, under the authority of scripture ('L'homme de
Dieu est avant tout l'homme de la Bible'—Spicq), teaches and refutes,
reforms and disciplines. He in particular must be *efficient* (ἄρτιος);
this word comes from the same root as *equipped* (ἐξηρτισμένος). Both
suggest a workman able to set his hand to any task that confronts him.
Good work is not used in the bad Pauline sense of 'works of law', but
denotes any of the useful tasks that fall to a minister's lot.

4c. **4:1–5.** THE WORK OF AN EVANGELIST. These verses continue
the previous section, and complete the author's charge to his
reader. He must preach and build up the Church, notwithstanding the resistance he will encounter.

1   *Before God, and before Christ Jesus*: one adverbial particle only in
the Greek, linking the two divine Persons very closely together.
Cp. in the Pastorals 1 Tim. 1:1; 2:5; 5:21 (with διαμαρτύρεσθαι, as
here); 6:13; 2 Tim. 1:2; Tit. 1:4; (2:13). Christ Jesus is described
as the one *who is to judge men living and dead* (cp. Acts 10:42; 1 Pet. 4:5);
that is, those who are alive at the time of his advent (see below), and
those who then are already dead. The invocation of the Judge adds
the greatest possible solemnity to the charge; Timothy will have to
give an account of the faithfulness of his ministry. *By his coming
appearance and his reign*: the construction changes abruptly (from
ἐνώπιον with the genitive to the simple accusative; cp. the use of this
case with the particles νή and μά). Christ's work as judge will take

living and dead, I adjure you by his coming appearance and
2 his reign, proclaim the message, press it home on all occasions,¹ convenient or inconvenient, use argument, reproof,
and appeal, with all the patience that the work of teaching
3 requires. For the time will come when they will not stand

¹ *Or* be on duty at all times.

---

place at his advent and will precede his reign. His 'coming appearance'
(ἐπιφάνεια) is referred to at 1 Tim. 6:14; 2 Tim. 1:10 (of the *first*
advent); 4:1, 8; Tit. 2:13; elsewhere in the New Testament this
word is used only at 2 Thess. 2:8, the word 'coming' (παρουσία)
being preferred. The word characteristic of the Pastorals may have
been chosen because of associations in religious and quasi-religious
usage elsewhere. It denotes the self-manifestation of a divine being,
with appropriate signs of majesty and power. It thus goes closely with
'reign', being Christ's glorious and manifest entry upon his kingdom.
It is in this light that Timothy must view his laborious, disappointing,
and frustrating duties.

2   *Proclaim the message.* The work is that of a herald (cp. 1 Tim. 2:7;
2 Tim. 1:11); and in truth Timothy is a herald (though an unprivi-
leged one—see the notes on these passages) of the King whose coming
has been spoken of in v. 1. The message (λόγος) which Timothy must
proclaim is found, for example, in the 'faithful saying (λόγος)' of
1 Tim. 1:15, 'Christ Jesus came into the world to save sinners'. This
is the Gospel (v. 5), and it is not a matter that can wait for convenient
occasions only. It is so important that *on all occasions, convenient or
inconvenient* (it is not clear whether the convenience of the preacher or
of his audience is considered; probably both) Timothy must *press it
home.* In Greek the verb (ἐπίστηθι) has no object, and it may therefore (see margin) have a sense sometimes found in the papyri, *be on
duty* (or, on guard). With 'mind' or some such word as object, the
verb means 'pay attention', and, though the object is wanting, this
sense may be intended here: 'pay attention (sc. to the work of
preaching) at all times . . .'. But the translation in the text is better.
    Preaching takes many forms. *Use argument, reproof, and appeal.*
'Argument' (cp. 1 Tim. 5:20) is not simply the logical argument
that appeals to the mind, but conviction of the conscience (cp.
John 16:8, where the same verb, ἐλέγχειν, is used). The preacher
must be prepared to use any available method, and to practise them
all with unwearied *patience.* His work will not grow easier, but harder.

3 *For the time will come* (and readers of the Epistle doubtless knew well
that it had already come) *when they will not stand wholesome teaching.*

wholesome teaching, but will follow their own fancy and
4 gather a crowd of teachers to tickle their ears. They will stop
5 their ears to the truth and turn to mythology. But you your-

---

It might be better to say '*the* wholesome teaching' (the Greek has
the article). Cp. 1 Tim. 1:10; the author is thinking of orthodox
Christian doctrine. Those whom he censures evidently do not wish
to cease to be, or to call themselves, Christians, but they desire
to have their own brand of Christianity. They *will follow their own
fancy and gather a crowd of teachers to tickle their ears*. The process of
Christian 'argument, reproof, and appeal' (v. 2) is offensive because
it afflicts the conscience; it is far more comfortable to secure a supply
of teachers who can be trusted to say only what their audience desire
to hear. It is possible in this way to maintain the outward form of
4 religion while denying its reality (3:5). Thus men *stop their ears to
the truth and turn to mythology* (literally, 'the myths'). For these myths
cp. 1 Tim. 1:4; 4:7; Tit. 1:14. In these circumstances, Timothy's
5 duty is clear: *You yourself* (σὺ δέ, as at 3:10, 14) *must keep calm and sane
at all times*. The answer to the new threat is simply to persevere in the
old task. It will not be easy; therefore *face hardship*: better, perhaps,
'accept hardship'. Enduring hardship is not an end in itself but in-
cidental to the main purpose: *work to spread the Gospel*, literally, 'Do
the work of an evangelist'. The word evangelist (εὐαγγελιστής) is
used at Eph. 4:11 (along with apostle, prophet, pastor, and teacher)
to describe a particular kind of worker in the Church. In Acts 21:8
Philip is described as 'the evangelist'. Like others, this term seems to
have been partly a description of an aspect of Christian work, partly a
technical name for a Church worker. It did not establish itself in
regular usage, perhaps because it was so evidently the duty of every
Christian to 'spread the Gospel' that the existence of a special class
of 'evangelists' would have seemed otiose; in particular, it may be
assumed that all ministers, whatever other designation they may bear,
are evangelists.

The next clause invites a similar comment. In *do all the duties of
your calling* the last word is misleading. It has nothing to do with the
idea of 'call', but renders διακονία, ministry or service. To this abstract
noun corresponds the term διάκονος, minister or deacon (see note on
1 Tim. 3:8). Unlike 'evangelist', this word did come into technical
use to describe not merely a minister but, eventually, a particular
class of ministers, although equally with evangelizing, service (in
various forms) is pre-eminently the duty of all Christians. To say this
is not to deny the undoubted truth that God calls certain men to the
special responsibility of making the fundamental pattern of evangelizing

self must keep calm and sane at all times; face hardship, work
to spread the Gospel, and do all the duties of your calling.

6   As for me, already my life is being poured out on the altar,
7   and the hour for my departure is upon me. I have run the

---

and service particularly clear. Such a man was Timothy, and it is
for him to carry out his responsibilities to the full (πληροφόρησον).
Cp. 1 Tim. 4:6.

5. 4: 6–18. PAUL

The remainder of the Epistle contains those parts of the Pastorals which may with the greatest plausibility be ascribed to
Paul himself; see Introduction, pp. 10 ff. There is nothing
here that Paul could not have written, and much that could
scarcely have been invented. When and where these sentences
were written, and whether they all belong to the same time and
place, are questions that can be answered only in terms of conjecture. See further below; also, in addition to Commentaries,
P. N. Harrison, *The Problem of the Pastoral Epistles* (1921),
pp. 87–135; *New Testament Studies*, ii (1956), 250–61.

5a. 4: 6–8. THE END OF PAUL'S COURSE. This short paragraph
links the charge to Timothy with the personal material that
follows. Timothy must be a 'good servant of Jesus Christ' because the apostle himself has now come to the end of his labours
and can do no more to spread the Gospel and serve the Church.

6   *As for me* brings out an emphatic personal pronoun; the Greek also
contains a conjunction (γάρ) which connects this verse with what
precedes it, and thus gives the ground of the exhortation in vv. 1–5.
Paul speaks of his death under the image of a drink-offering (cp.
Phil. 2:17); it is, however, the context rather than the word itself
that suggests martyrdom.

The hour for my departure is upon me—is in fact so close that Paul can
speak of the offering of his life in the present tense.

7   *I have run the great race.* See note on 1 Tim. 6:12. There is much to
be said for the view that here the two related metaphors of the
wrestling-match and the race are used together: I have fought the
good fight, *I have finished the course.* The meaning is in any case clear:
Paul's work is done, and well done. *I have kept faith*: the Greek has the
article, and we should perhaps render, '*the* faith'. This might be understood as the doctrinal content of Christianity ('the Christian faith'),

8 great race, I have finished the course, I have kept faith. And
   now the prize awaits me, the garland of righteousness which
   the Lord, the all-just Judge, will award me on that great
   Day; and it is not for me alone, but for all who have set their
   hearts on his coming appearance.

10   Do your best to join me soon; for Demas has deserted me

---

or perhaps as the deposit entrusted to apostle and minister (1 Tim.
6:20; 2 Tim. 1:12, 14). The word πίστις can mean pledge, or oath,
and it is an interesting suggestion that it here continues the metaphor
of the first part of the verse, and refers to the oath taken by a con-
testant in the games. Paul has 'kept the rules' (2:5).

After victorious conflict, *the prize awaits me*. *The garland* is primarily
a sign of victory, but is also (see Spicq) a mark of immortality. It is a
garland *of righteousness* probably in the sense of a reward for righteousness; it would not be impossible to take it as a reward consisting in
righteousness, the righteousness of Christ which is graciously bestowed on sinful man, but this is not so suitable to the context; though
the righteousness which is rewarded is in the first instance God's gift.
On that great Day, that is, judgement day, when the Lord comes. This
reference to the *parousia* shows that by *the Lord, the all-just Judge*, is
meant Christ. For *his coming appearance* see note on v. 1. *Set their hearts
on* correctly explains 'loved' (ἠγαπηκόαι). Men will desire the coming
of Christ only if they are prepared, by the divine gift of righteousness,
to meet him; if they are so prepared they may expect to share Paul's
reward, which is not for him *alone*.

5*b*. **4:9–18.** PERSONAL INFORMATION AND COMMISSIONS. For the
question whether these verses may be regarded as a genuine
Pauline fragment see Introduction, pp. 10 ff., and the detailed
notes below. Many Pauline letters end with a paragraph such
as this; cp. Rom. 15:19–16:23; 1 Cor. 16:5–18; Phil. 4:10–20;
Col. 4:7–17; not 1 Timothy.

9   Timothy is asked to *join* Paul *soon* (ταχέως). In Acts 17:14 Paul
departs hurriedly from Beroea leaving Timothy (and Silas) behind.
On his arrival at Athens (17:15) he sends word back to Beroea that
his colleagues are to join him as soon as possible (ὡς τάχιστα). It seems
that a little later (1 Thess. 3:2–6) Paul sent Timothy to Macedonia,
and was delighted by his return with good news. Timothy was also
sent to Corinth (1 Cor. 4:17; 16:10). The first of these occasions
might at first sight supply a good context for the present message,

because his heart was set on this world; he has gone to Thes-
11 salonica, Crescens to Galatia,[1] Titus to Dalmatia; I have no
one with me but Luke. Pick up Mark and bring him with you,
12 for I find him a useful assistant. Tychicus I have sent to

[1] *Or* Gaul; *some witnesses read* Gallia.

---

but all are inconsistent with the preceding paragraph, which speaks
of Paul's death as imminent. It must be remembered, however, that
these verses, if genuine at all, were not necessarily all written at the
same time.

10   *Demas has deserted me.* Cp. Col. 4:14; Philem. 24. Demas's defection
is presumably subsequent to these references, though these were
probably (but not certainly) written in Rome towards the close of
Paul's life. Demas's *heart was set* (contrast v. 8) *on this world*; cp. 1 Tim.
6:17; Tit. 2:12 ('the present age'—but the Greek is the same).
Eschatological thought in the Pastorals is less rich and powerful than
in Paul's own letters, but it has not been abandoned. It is the age to
come that should determine the life of Christians. *He has gone to Thes-
salonica*; not necessarily as an apostate; possibly to work a more
comfortable mission field. *Crescens* is not mentioned elsewhere in the
New Testament. If he went to *Galatia* he was presumably revisiting
a Pauline mission field (Acts 16:6; 18:23; Gal. 1:2; 4:13; &c.); if
he went to *Gaul* (margin; a well-attested variant, and one that might
naturally have been altered by copyists to the more familiar Galatia)
he was probably breaking new ground, perhaps on the way to Spain
(cp. Rom. 15:24, 28). It should be noted that with some Greek
writers the name Galatia means Gaul.

   Titus in the epistle that bears his name has been left in Crete (Tit.
1:5). *Dalmatia* is not mentioned elsewhere in the New Testament.
11   *Luke.* Cp. Col. 4:14; Philem. 24, and see the note above on Demas.
Luke was apparently with Paul in Rome; cp. Acts 28:16 ('*We*
entered Rome').

   Pick up Mark and bring him with you. Presumably Mark was to be
found somewhere on Timothy's route as he travelled to join Paul.
Mark is mentioned by Paul at Col. 4:10; Philem. 24. Acts 12:25;
13:13 belong to an earlier period. A probable though not quite
certain meaning of 1 Pet. 5:13 is that Mark eventually reached Rome.
It must not be regarded as certain that all these passages refer to the
same person; Mark was a common name. *A useful assistant* conceals
the word 'ministry' (διακονία); see note on v. 5. It is not implied that
Mark was a deacon in the technical sense (διάκονος); he was useful
for Christian service.
12   *Tychicus I have sent to Ephesus*; so Eph. 6:21; cp. Col. 4:7. See also

13 Ephesus. When you come, bring the cloak I left with Carpus at Troas, and the books, above all my notebooks.

14   Alexander the copper-smith did me a great deal of harm.
15 Retribution will fall upon him from the Lord. You had better be on your guard against him too, for he violently
16 opposed everything I said. At the first hearing of my case no

---

Acts 20:4 (Tychicus accompanies Paul on the way to Jerusalem); Tit. 3:12.

13   One more of Paul's assistants is mentioned: *Carpus*, who is *at Troas*. Nothing else is known of him. Troas is mentioned at Acts 16:8, 11; 20:5 f.; 2 Cor. 2:12. *Cloak*: the Latin *paenula*, a heavy outer garment. It is perhaps reasonable to conjecture that these words (if genuine) were written as winter drew on; it is, however, to be noted that the word in question could mean a cloth for wrapping, or a case for containing, books; see the latter part of the verse.

The books, above all my notebooks. If this translation is adopted, 'the books' will probably be copies of the (Old Testament) scriptures; cp. Luke 4:17, 20; Gal. 3:10. 'The notebooks' are literally parchments (μεμβράνας, a Latin loan-word), perhaps (in view of the previous reference to books) not yet made up into rolls, and thus Paul's own writing material. But it is against this view that it is very unlikely that anyone would make notes on the very expensive parchment rather than on the common papyrus. It may be that official documents of some kind (possibly proving Paul's citizenship) are meant; or 'books' may mean writings of any kind ('possibly copies of his own correspondence'—Lock), 'parchments' Biblical books.

14   *Alexander the copper-smith* cannot be certainly identified. In the Ephesian riot a leading part was played by Demetrius the silver-smith (Acts 19:24), and in the same context an Alexander is mentioned (19:33), but there is no reason to connect the present Alexander (another common name) with this event. 1 Tim. 1:20 is a better parallel, but in no way conclusive. Presumably Alexander was to be found in a locality where Timothy might expect to meet him. *Did me a great deal of harm*; cp. Gen. 50:15, 17. A possible but less likely rendering is 'preferred serious charges against me'. *Retribution will fall upon him from the Lord* recalls several passages in both Testaments (e.g. Ps.
15 62:12; Prov. 24:12; Rom. 2:6; 2 Cor 11:15). Alexander's violent opposition might be that of a heathen, but could equally be that of a heretical Christian; cp. 1 Tim. 1:20.

16   In the present context (cp. v. 6) *the first hearing of my case* suggests

A customer at a wine shop displays his cloak (2 Tim. 4:13).

one came into court to support me; they all left me in the
17 lurch; I pray that it may not be held against them. But the
Lord stood by me and lent me strength, so that I might
be his instrument in making the full proclamation of the
Gospel for the whole pagan world to hear; and thus I was
18 rescued out of the lion's jaws. And the Lord will rescue me

---

a trial in Rome, and 'first' has often been taken to imply that the
Pastorals assume an acquittal (v. 17), and subsequent ministry,
whether in Spain or in the East. It is possible, however, that if this

A procession of magistrates, from a fourth-century relief in Aquileia.
1 Tim. 2:2; 2 Tim. 4:16.

verse comes from a genuine fragment the reference is to an earlier
trial. For the wholesale desertion mentioned in this verse cp. 1:15
('everyone in the province of Asia deserted me'). *I pray that it may not
be held against them* recalls Luke 23:34; Acts 7:60; both verses may
have been known to the author of 2 Timothy, both incidents to Paul
himself.

17   Deserted by men, Paul was not forsaken by the Lord. *I was rescued
out of the lion's jaws* probably means release, but need not do so, since
making the full proclamation of the Gospel for the whole pagan world to hear
(or, 'fulfilling my own ministry of preaching . . .') could refer to witness
18 borne when on trial before the ruler of the whole pagan world. This is
confirmed by the next verse, for the margin (*. . . and bring me safely into*

from every attempt to do me harm, and keep me safe until
his heavenly reign begins.[1] Glory to him for ever and ever!
Amen.

19   Greetings to Prisca and Aquila, and the household of
Onesiphorus.

20   Erastus stayed behind at Corinth, and I left Trophimus ill
21 at Miletus. Do try to get here before winter.

Greetings from Eubulus, Pudens, Linus, and Claudia, and
from all the brotherhood here.

[1] *Or* from all that evil can do, and bring me safely into his heavenly
kingdom.

---

his heavenly kingdom) is probably correct. The text seems to imply the
belief that Paul will survive till the *parousia*; such a belief Paul may
once have held (1 Thess. 4:17; 1 Cor. 15:51 f.), though possibly not
at the end of his career (Phil. 1:21).
Glory to him. . . . Cp. 1 Tim. 1:17.

6. 4: 19–22. FINAL GREETINGS
This short section is cast in a form characteristic of the
Pauline letters, e.g. Rom. 16:3–16, 21 ff.

19   *Greetings to Prisca and Aquila*; for these two cp. Acts 18:2, 18, 26;
Rom. 16:3; 1 Cor. 16:19. In Acts they are found in Ephesus; so also
in 1 Corinthians. Rom. 16:3 implies that they are in Rome, unless
the view is accepted that Rom. 16 was originally sent to Ephesus.
2 Timothy is ostensibly written from Rome, and the two should thus
be thought of as having returned to Ephesus (where perhaps Timothy
is supposed to be stationed), or as having migrated elsewhere. But if
this verse is genuine it need not have been written in Rome.
Onesiphorus also had been in both Rome and Ephesus; see 1:16 ff.

20   *Erastus*: cp. Acts 19:22; Rom. 16:23, which may not, however,
refer to the same person. In the former passage an Erastus is sent
from Ephesus to Macedonia; in the latter, Erastus is probably the
borough treasurer of Corinth, not necessarily a travelling assistant of Paul's. The *Trophimus* of Acts 20:4; 21:29 was an Ephesian.

21   *Do try to get here before winter*. Cp. v. 9.
Eubulus, Pudens, Linus, and Claudia are not mentioned elsewhere in
the New Testament. According to Eusebius (*Hist. Eccl.* III. ii. 1; III.
iv. 9; v. vi. 1), and other sources, Linus was the name of the bishop of
Rome who immediately succeeded Peter.

22   The Lord be with your spirit. Grace be with you all!

---

22   *The Lord be with your spirit. Grace be with you all!* 'Your' is singular, retaining the form of a private letter; 'you' is plural, and recognizes that the letter was in fact destined for public use. 'All', which is not in the Greek, is no doubt intended to indicate this. The 'grace' is in the usual Pauline form. For 'your spirit' cp. Gal. 6:18; Phil. 4:23; Philem. 25.

TITUS

1 FROM Paul, servant of God and apostle of Jesus Christ,
marked as such by faith and knowledge and hope—the faith
of God's chosen people, knowledge of the truth as our re-
2 ligion has it, and the hope of eternal life.[1] Yes, it is eternal
3 life that God, who cannot lie, promised long ages ago, and
now in his own good time he has openly declared himself in

[1] *Or* apostle of Jesus Christ, to bring God's chosen people to faith and to
a knowledge of the truth as our religion has it, with its hope for eternal life.

---

1. 1: 1–4. ADDRESS

See the notes on 1 Tim. 1:1 f.; 2 Tim. 1:1 f.; the address in
this Epistle is longer, but contains many parallels with those in
the other letters, and only fresh points will be noted.

1 *Servant of God* is not in 1 or 2 Timothy, but resembles the Pauline
phrase 'Servant of Christ Jesus'; cp. Rom. 1:1; Phil. 1:1. In the
Pastorals cp. 2 Tim. 2:24.

The description of Paul is joined to the following phrases by the
preposition κατά (literally, 'according to'). This may be taken (as in
the text) to add to the description of Paul himself, or (as in the
margin) to describe the purpose of his apostleship. The rendering in
the text is better (cp. the use of κατά in Tit. 1:3, 4, 9; 3:5, 7), though
it scarcely expresses the full sense. Paul is not merely *marked as*, shown
to be, an *apostle . . . by the faith of God's chosen people, knowledge of the*
2 *truth as our religion has it, and the hope of eternal life*; his apostleship is constituted and determined by this *faith, knowlege*, and *hope*. For 'knowledge of the truth' cp. 1 Tim. 2:4; 2 Tim. 2:25; 3:7. 'Religion' is a
common word in the Pastorals; see note on 1 Tim. 2:2. The ultimate
aim at which Paul's apostleship points is eternal life; it looks beyond
present suffering (cp. 2 Tim. 2:4 f.) to the purpose which God ordained in the beginning and will manifest at the end. The faithfulness
of God (cp. 2 Tim. 2:13) is here negatively expressed: he *cannot lie*,
and his promises may therefore be trusted.

The full realization of eternal life is a matter of hope (cp. 3:7, and
3 note); but this does not mean that God is not active and knowable
in the present. *Now in his own good time* (cp. Gal. 4:4) *he has openly*

the proclamation which was entrusted to me by ordinance of God our Saviour.

4   To Titus, my true-born son in the faith which we share, grace and peace from God our Father and Christ Jesus our Saviour.

5   My intention in leaving you behind in Crete was that you

---

declared himself; but it would be better to keep closer to the admittedly somewhat clumsy Greek and say: he has manifested his word. The writer is probably thinking not of the personal Word of God who became flesh (John 1:14), but of the revealed truth, the message or Gospel which is expressed *in the proclamation* of apostles and evangelists. The word (λόγος) is a common New Testament term for the divine proclamation spoken first by Jesus himself (e.g. Mark 2:2) and subsequently by those who bore witness to him (e.g. Acts 4:4). It is true that in this proclamation God himself is present, but it is an important truth that it is in and by his word that God reveals himself. Paul was *entrusted* with this proclamation *by ordinance of God our Saviour*: cp. 1 Tim. 1:1 (where 'command' translates the same Greek as 'ordinance'), and the note.

4   It is *the faith which we* (Paul the Jew and Titus the Gentile— Gal. 2:3; or perhaps the pronoun refers to all Christians) *share* that makes Titus Paul's *true-born son*, just as it makes Paul an apostle.

Grace and peace. Alone among the Pastorals Titus omits 'mercy', and thereby agrees with all the genuine Pauline letters.

2. 1:5–16. DEVELOPMENT OF CHRISTIAN WORK IN CRETE

Titus's first task in Crete is to appoint Church leaders. Among their duties will be that of confuting objectors. This controversial work is important because of the opposition that exists, arising partly out of the notoriously bad character of the Cretans themselves, and partly out of the activities of Jewish gnostics. These Titus must himself resist, and the paragraph ends with a short example of the way in which error is to be refuted and heretics dealt with.

5   *Crete*: see Introduction, p. 9. Paul touched at Crete on his voyage to Rome (Acts 27:7 f.); the reference in this Epistle implies another visit, including a period (though a brief one) of missionary activity, which it is impossible to fit into the *known* work of Paul.

Set in order what was left over describes the task awaiting Titus in a

should set in order what was left over, and in particular should institute elders in each town. In doing so, observe the tests I

---

scantily worked mission field; it is, however, not wrong to add that it describes the situation of the Church as a whole at the time when

Church of St. Titus, Gortyna, Crete (sixth or eighth century). Tit. 1:5.

the Pastorals were written. Paul was dead, and not a few things were 'left over', with the result that Paul's assistants and successors inherited the tasks he had not completed. 'The building of the Church is not a work so easy that it can be brought all at once to perfection' (Calvin).

One of the tasks 'left over' at the end of Paul's career was the supply of ministers to the Church. This general situation is probably in mind in the following instructions for Titus's work in Crete. He must *institute elders in each town.* For elders see Introduction, pp. 31 f., and notes on 1 Tim 4:14; 5:17–22. For the general requirements laid on ministers see 1 Tim. 3:2–13. The present passage is similar. In neither is any rule laid down for the *manner* in which ministers are to be appointed, and the fact that Titus is told to institute them does not

6 prescribed: is he a man of unimpeachable character, faithful
to his one wife,[1] the father of children who are believers,
who are under no imputation of loose living, and are not out
7 of control? For as God's steward a bishop must be a man
of unimpeachable character. He must not be overbearing
or short-tempered; he must be no drinker, no brawler, no
8 money-grubber, but hospitable, right-minded, temperate,

[1] *See note on 1 Timothy 3: 2.*

---

6 mean that the congregation was to play no part. For *a man of unimpeachable character* cp. v. 7, and 1 Tim. 3:10 (ἀνέγκλητος in each, though
the translation differs); also 1 Tim. 3:2; 5:7; 6:14 (where the Greek
is ἀνεπίλημπτος). *Faithful to his one wife*: cp. 1 Tim. 3:2, 12. *The father
of children . . . not out of control*: there are similar requirements regarding
ministers' households in 1 Tim. 3:4, 12. The author of the Pastorals
is very concerned that no moral failure in, or connected with, the
ministry should prejudice the Church's witness.

7 *A bishop.* For this word see Introduction, p. 32, and note on 1 Tim.
3:2. As *for* (γάρ) shows, 'bishop' here has the same meaning as 'elder'
(v. 5). The change from plural (elders) to singular (bishop) is best
accounted for not by supposing that in each town there was a group
of elders but only one bishop, but by the view (see especially F. J. A.
Hort, *The Christian Ecclesia* (1914), p. 191) that whereas *elder* describes
an official, *bishop* describes his function: The elders you appoint must
have certain qualifications, for a man who exercises oversight must
be. . . . For a comparable change in number cp. 1 Tim. 2:15; and for
the view that the Pastorals disclose two different ways of ordering the
Church see G. Bornkamm in *T.W.N.T.* vi. 667 f.

As God's Steward: cp. 1 Cor. 4:1. Steward (οἰκονόμος) recalls the
fact that the Pastorals speak of the Church as God's house or household (οἶκος, οἰκία: 1 Tim. 3:15; cp. 2 Tim. 2:20; also 1 Tim. 3:5,
12; 5:4).

Not overbearing. The word is not used in 1 Tim. 3, though the sense
of it is to be found there. Stubborn perverseness that will not admit
error is in mind. *No drinker, no brawler*: cp. 1 Tim. 3:3. *No money-
grubber*: cp. 1 Tim. 3:3, 8; 6:10; 2 Tim. 3:2. It is the sordidness of
making profit out of Christian service, rather than dishonest gain,
8 that is here condemned. *Hospitable*: cp. 1 Tim. 3:2. *Right-minded*:
the word (φιλάγαθος) is not used elsewhere in the New Testament;
literally, loving the good. It is common in adulatory inscriptions.
Temperate: cp. 1 Tim. 3:2. *Just*: δίκαιος, but here the word does not

9 just, devout, and self-controlled. He must adhere to the true
doctrine, so that he may be well able both to move his
hearers with wholesome teaching and to confute objectors.

10   There are all too many, especially among Jewish converts,

---

have its Pauline theological sense. *Devout*: cp. 1 Tim. 2:8, where the
translation is different. *Self-controlled*: the adjective is not used elsewhere in the New Testament, but cp. Acts 24:25; 1 Cor. 7:9; 9:25;
Gal. 5:23; 2 Pet. 1:6.

9   *The true doctrine* is literally 'the faithful word (or saying) which is in
accordance with the teaching', and thus recalls the 'faithful sayings'
(see note on 1 Tim. 1:15). These are to be believed and accepted not
because the Church is able by some authority of its own to accredit
certain doctrines and reject others; behind the faithful sayings lies
God's faithfulness, because of which the Church may trust them and
build its doctrine upon them. The minister must be well grounded
in Christian doctrine ('for the Church cannot be governed in any
other way than by the word'—Calvin), both that he may teach the
faithful, and deal with adversaries—*to move his hearers with wholesome
teaching and to confute objectors*. For the activity of the presbyter-bishop
in teaching cp. 1 Tim. 5:17. For *wholesome* (healthy) *teaching* cp.
1 Tim. 1:10; 6:3; 2 Tim. 1:13; 4:3; Tit. 1:9, 13; 2:1, 2, 8. The word
suggests not only freedom from error, but also teaching which is able
to impart healthiness, that is, salvation (cp. 2:11). *Confute* ($\dot{\epsilon}\lambda\dot{\epsilon}\gamma\chi\epsilon\iota\nu$)
means to expose, and by exposing, convict. Those who contradict
the truth must be shown their errors, whether they accept the demonstration or not. Cp. 1 Tim. 5:20; 2 Tim. 4:2; Tit. 1:13; 2:15,
where the same word appears under a variety of translations. The
objectors are not outside the Church, but within it; the author would
not have found it necessary to deal with the heathen in this way.
      There is no doubt of the need for the bishop's controversial powers.

10   *There are all too many* who need his attention. They are *out of all control*,
that is, they are Christians who have gone astray rather than heathen
(see above, and cp. the use of the same word in v. 6). Elsewhere in
the Pastorals (see 1 Tim. 4:1; 2 Tim. 3:1) such men are spoken of
as constituting an evil still to come in the future (relative to the time
of Paul); here the historical mask slips, and they appear as contem-
poraries of the writer. The disorderly, who *talk wildly and lead men's
minds astray* are to be found *especially among Jewish converts*; literally,
'those of the circumcision'. See further note on v. 14. The Jewish
danger is now different from what it was in Paul's time. There is
ample evidence for the existence of Jews in Crete, and the fact that

who are out of all control; they talk wildly and lead men's
11 minds astray. Such men must be curbed, because they are
ruining whole families by teaching things they should not, and
12 all for sordid gain. It was a Cretan prophet, one of their own
countrymen, who said, 'Cretans were always liars, vicious

---

it is in this Epistle that Jewish opponents are specifically mentioned
probably reflects the circle in which it was intended to be read.

11   *Such men must be curbed*, or perhaps 'muzzled', 'silenced'. Sharp
disciplinary action is intended (cp. v. 13), both for the safety of the
community, and also for the ultimate good of the offender. *They are
ruining whole families* recalls 2 Tim. 3:6, but goes further. The kind
of mental and moral disaster in mind is suggested by v. 15. *Teaching
things they should not*; see v. 14. It is characteristic of the author that he
does not go into details regarding false doctrine; he sees its results
and that it ought not to exist; and then denounces rather than refutes
it. No doubt he was wise. To have pursued the devious ways of gnostic
mythology would have suited those who delighted in them, and done
no good to the Church. The false teachers are said to act *all for sordid
gain*; this underlines the requirement of v. 7. One who regards
ecclesiastical office as a means of making money will be particularly
liable to trim his teaching by anything but the truth.

12   The introduction of *Cretans* is not easy to understand after the reference in v. 10 to Jewish converts. Either the author has not fully
thought through his material (cp. 'Jewish myths' in v. 14), or the Jews
are to be thought of as in great measure assimilated to Cretan life,
so that the heretics can be chastised with both sticks, one provided
by the Cretan prophet, the other by the Old Testament.

A Cretan prophet, one of their own countrymen: almost certainly Epi-
menedes of Crete (6th–5th century B.C.), though part of the hexameter
line was taken over by Callimachus of Cyrene (3rd century B.C.),
to whom some of the Fathers attributed the whole. In what sense is he
described as a prophet? He was certainly looked upon as having foretold the future (see the story in Plato, *Laws* i. 642D; cp. Cicero, *de
Divinatione*, i. xviii. 34), though Aristotle says that his oracles were
rather about obscure events in the past than about events still to
come (*Rhetoric*, III. xvii. 10; 1418a). By speaking of him as a prophet,
however, the New Testament does not place him with Isaiah and
Jeremiah, but with Caiaphas (John 11:51; and, as Spicq suggests,
with Balaam's ass; but cp. also Calvin: 'From this passage we may
infer that those persons are superstitious, who do not venture to borrow

13 brutes, lazy gluttons'—and he told the truth! All the more
   reason why you should pull them up sharply, so that they
14 may come to a sane belief, instead of lending their ears to
   Jewish myths and commandments of merely human origin,
   the work of men who turn their backs upon the truth.

15   To the pure all things are pure; but nothing is pure to the

---

13 anything from heathen authors'). *He told the truth,* though he did not
   himself see the full significance of what he said.
        Cretans were always liars—hence they 'lead men's minds astray'
   (v. 10); *vicious brutes*—and thus 'out of all control' (v. 10); *lazy
   gluttons*—hence their love of 'sordid gain' (v. 11). Gentle treatment is
   of no use with such men. You must *pull them up sharply* (v. 9; cp. 2 Cor.
   13:10), and that for their own good. Severe disease calls for severe
   remedies, that 'they may be healthy in the faith'—*may come to a sane
14 belief.* The error from which they must be rescued is that of *lending their
   ears to Jewish myths and commandments of merely human origin* (cp. Mark
   7:7), *the work of men who turn their backs upon the truth.* For 'myths' see
   note on 1 Tim. 1:4; also 4:7; 2 Tim. 4:4. That they are here qualified as Jewish is an important pointer to their character, though it
   must not be assumed that the word bears precisely the same meaning
   wherever it occurs. The 'truth' which is contradicted by 'commandments of merely human origin' is evidently the truth of scripture. The
   commandments were apparently ascetic, representing a combination
   of Jewish food laws and dualistic rejection of the material (cp. Col.
15 2:21 f.), since they are corrected by the statement, *To the pure all
   things are pure.* This recalls Mark 7:18–23 (cp. Luke 11:41); Rom.
   14:14, 20; but the thought here is not identical with that of the other
   passages. It lacks the force, clarity, and precision of the Pauline
   argument. 'Pure' when first used (taking the English order) must
   have an ethical and spiritual sense (pure in heart); in the next use, it
   is ceremonial; that is, to the morally good, all things (foods) are permitted. The next occurrence of 'pure' is again fundamentally ceremonial (since the heretics in question do in fact deny that for them
   the articles under consideration are pure—permitted), but the corresponding word 'tainted' again swings round to a moral and
   intellectual sense—*tainted alike in reason and conscience.* Paul's argument
   (in Rom. 14; cp. also Mark 7:19) is that all things are pure, but that
   it is harmful to eat what is itself pure with a bad conscience, or to the
   detriment of one's weaker Christian brother; the strong (who know
   the truth) must accommodate their practice to the needs of the weak.
   In Titus, it is the weak (in the sense of Rom. 14 and 15) who are not

tainted minds of disbelievers, tainted alike in reason and con-
16 science. They profess to acknowledge God, but deny him by
their actions. Their detestable obstinacy disqualifies them
for any good work.

2   For your own part, what you say must be in keeping with

---

protected but attacked; their reason and conscience are defiled, and
this inward defilement corrupts their food and makes it *to them* unclean
—though in truth it is pure. Their *reason* is tainted, because they do
not grasp the truth that 'everything that God created is good, and
[that] nothing is to be rejected' (1 Tim. 4:4), and their *conscience* is
tainted (not weak) in that (as the next verse shows) they are hypocritically professing to be religious whereas their abstinence is not
supported by positive goodness. Naturally, it must be remembered
that the abstainers of Tit. 1 were different people from those of Rom.
14 and 15.

16   That *they profess to acknowledge God* (or, better, 'that they know
God') indicates the gnostic tendency of the heretics. Their claim (in
oratio recta) is, We know God (cp. 1 John 2:4). It is true, as some
commentators point out, that this claim could also be Jewish, but
it seems to be a Jewish kind of gnosticism with which we are dealing.
The New Testament always rejects such specious claims, insisting
that God is known in Jesus Christ, and that knowledge is attested by
obedience. Hence it can be said of those who are tainted in conscience
that, whatever claims they may make, they *deny* God *by their actions*.

Detestable may be ironical; the heretics would regard unclean food
as detestable (βδελυκτός, abominable). Because they are *obstinate*
(disobedient, or unbelieving) they lose the power to do *any good work*.

3. 2:1–3:2. THE WAY OF CHRISTIAN OBEDIENCE

The previous paragraph closed with the picture of men who
because of their obstinate disobedience are unfit to produce any
good work. The faithful Christian, on the contrary, will offer
his obedience to God. But how will he express it? The new
section gives instructions through Titus for the whole community; the 'household rules' given in certain other epistles
(Eph. 5:22–6:9; Col. 3:18–4:1; 1 Pet. 2:18–3:9) are recalled.
Older men, older women, younger women, and younger men
are first dealt with; then slaves. The next sub-section digresses
to recall the goodness of God in his redemption of the world in
order to present the *ground* of Christian obedience; and finally
the author turns to the duties of Christians to society. Three times,

2 wholesome doctrine. Let the older men know that they should
   be sober, high-principled, and temperate, sound in faith, in
3 love, and in endurance. The older women, similarly, should
   be reverent in their bearing, not scandal-mongers or slaves to
4 strong drink; they must set a high standard, and school the

---

in 2:5, 8, 10, he lays emphasis on the impression Christian life
should make upon onlookers; 2:14 and 3:2 are similar. He
evidently valued this impression, and there can be little doubt
that it proved eventually to be one of the strongest missionary
forces.

3a. **2:1–8. OLDER MEN AND WOMEN: YOUNGER MEN AND WOMEN.**
It is a characteristic feature of the 'household rules' in Titus
that the congregation is divided by age and sex, not by family relationships. The moral claims laid upon rank-and-file Christians
are substantially the same as those made elsewhere upon
ministers. There is only one standard, though it is perhaps
especially important that official and public persons should
reach it.

1   Others may by their actions deny the God whom they profess to
know; Titus must not do so. For *wholesome doctrine* cp. 1:9 ('wholesome teaching', but the Greek is the same).

2   The qualities requisite in *older men* are described in language
characteristic of the Pastorals. For *sober* see 1 Tim. 3:2, 11; *high-
principled*, 1 Tim. 3:8, 11; *temperate*, 1 Tim. 3:2; Tit. 1:8; 2:5; cp.
1 Tim. 2:9, 15; 2 Tim. 1:7; Tit. 2:4, 6, 12; *sound in faith*, Tit. 1:13;
for *love* connected with faith, 1 Tim. 1:5, 14; 2:15; 4:12; 6:11;
2 Tim. 1:13; 2:22; 3:10; for *endurance* see 1 Tim. 6:11; 2 Tim. 3:10
(in both these places the word is translated 'fortitude').

3   *The older women* are to show corresponding (*similarly*) virtues. Cp.
the instructions in 1 Tim. 2:9–15; 3:11; 5:9–14. The desire to
avoid any kind of scandal which might bring the Church into disrepute is evident. *Reverent in their bearing*; the word (ἱεροπρεπεῖς) has
a cultic background, but all the acts of a Christian are sacred. *They
must set a high standard* conceals the word καλοδιδάσκαλος; that is,
the older women must not simply set a good example but actually
teach the younger—in part, no doubt, but not wholly, by example.
Cp. 1 Tim. 2:12; it is their husbands that women must not teach.

4 The older women must *school the younger*; that is, teach them to be
temperate.

5 younger women to be loving wives and mothers, temperate,
chaste, and kind, busy at home, respecting the authority of
their own husbands. Thus the Gospel will not be brought
into disrepute.

, 7   Urge the younger men, similarly, to be temperate in all
things, and set them a good example yourself. In your teach-
8 ing, you must show integrity and high principle, and use
wholesome speech to which none can take exception. This
will shame any opponent, when he finds not a word to say to
our discredit.

For the virtues required of younger women cp. 1 Tim. 5:14, and
note the positive religious value which the author finds in the vocation
5 to marriage and child-bearing. The language used is paralleled in
many honorific inscriptions, i.e. the author considers the civic virtues
acknowledged in the Hellenistic world worthy of Christian imitation.
These virtues for the most part require no explanation. For *respecting
the authority of their own husbands* see 1 Tim. 2:12, and cp. 1 Cor. 11:3,
&c. *Thus the Gospel* (literally, and better, 'the word of God') *will not be
brought into disrepute.* This motive constantly recurs; doubtless there
was good reason why it should do so.
6   The social picture is completed by the addition of *the younger men.*
These too must be *temperate* (cp. vv. 2, 4, 5) *in all things.*
7   In the following clause one participle (παρεχόμενος) governs *yourself, example, integrity, high principle,* and *speech.* In general terms, Titus
must offer himself to the young men (it is implied that he too is
young; cp. Introduction, p. 10) as a good example; *in his teaching,*
since teaching is one of his main tasks, he must show special characteristics. 'High principle' (σεμνότης), with its cognate adjective, is
common in the Pastorals (1 Tim. 2:2; 3:4, 8, 11; Tit. 2:2); elsewhere
8 in the New Testament only at Phil. 4:8. For *wholesome speech* cp.
1 Tim. 1:10; 6:3; &c. *To which none can take exception* introduces
another expression of the author's anxiety for the good repute of
Christianity. Current accusations against Christians may be recalled;
e.g. Tacitus, *Annals,* xv. 44 (*per flagitia invisos*); Pliny, *Letters,* x. 96
(*superstitionem pravam immodicam*).

3*b.* **2:9, 10.** SLAVES. These form the only group in addition to
those based on sex and age. Cp. 1 Tim. 6:1 f., though these
verses may (see the notes) be addressed specifically to elders who

9   Tell slaves to respect their masters' authority in every-
     thing, and to comply with their demands without answering
10   back; not to pilfer, but to show themselves strictly honest
     and trustworthy; for in all such ways they will add lustre to
     the doctrine of God our Saviour.
11   For the grace of God has dawned upon the world with

---

are slaves. Note that it is to slaves that the author offers the
opportunity of adding lustre to the Christian profession.

9   Christian *slaves* constituted a special danger to the good repute
     of the Church. Their Christian freedom could if wrongly expressed
     lead to the opinion that they and their brethren were social revolu-
     tionaries. Accordingly they must be careful *to respect their masters'*
     authority in everything. The next words illustrate the requirement in
10   practical terms; *to comply with their demands without answering back; not to*
     pilfer, but to show themselves strictly honest and trustworthy. Such behaviour
     will secure not only a negative but a positive end: *they will add lustre to*
     the doctrine of God our Saviour. Nothing brings so much credit upon
     Christian doctrine as the quality of character it produces—slaves
     who are honest, and honestly seek to please their masters, for example.
     For 'God our Saviour' cp. 1 Tim. 1:1; 2:3; Tit. 1:3; 3:4; and see
     note on 2:13. Nothing in the present passage suggests that Christ
     is intended by the words. The genitive probably means not 'teaching
     about God our Saviour', but 'teaching which proceeds from him'.

3c. **2:11–3:2.** GRACE AND OBEDIENCE. Reference to God as
Saviour proves to be the point of departure for a digression,
which has the effect of rooting the ethical teaching of 2:1–3:2
in the doctrine of redemption on which the ethical requirements
are based. The connexion is obscured by the translation (v. 11)
of σωτήριος as *with healing*; this is not incorrect (see below), but
fails to bring out the fact that the word is cognate with Saviour
(σωτήρ, vv. 10, 13). It is because God is the Saviour that there
is grace and healing for mankind, and because Jesus sacrificed
himself for all mankind that old and young men, old and young
women, can be bidden to live in obedience to God.

11   For *the grace of God* in the Pastorals see 1 Tim. 1:14; 2 Tim. 1:9;
     2:1; Tit. 3:7. Here, though the verb *has dawned* (ἐπεφάνη; cp. 3:4,
     and the use of the cognate ἐπιφάνεια in 1 Tim. 6:14; 2 Tim. 1:10;
     4:1, 8; Tit. 2:13) is not Pauline, the thought is the Pauline thought

12 healing for all mankind; and by it we are disciplined to renounce godless ways and worldly desires, and to live a life
   of temperance, honesty, and godliness in the present age,
13 looking forward to the happy fulfilment of our hopes when

---

of the gracious activity of God which was put into effect in the
historic mission of Jesus Christ. *With healing for all mankind*; more
literally, 'salvation'—the word is cognate with 'Saviour' in vv. 10,
13, &c., and with 'salvation' in 2 Tim. 2:10; 3:15. In secular Greek
the word is sometimes used to describe the beneficial results of medical
care, and 'healing' is here a suitable metaphorical rendering, though
it unfortunately obscures the verbal connexion with the other passages
mentioned. What God has done for men in Christ he has done with
a view to their restoration to total health. He has done it *for all mankind*; cp. 1 Tim. 2:4, 6. Thus, he has done it for slaves (vv. 9 f.).

The author diverges further from Pauline usage when he adds that
12 by this grace *we are disciplined*. In Paul grace is not educative, but
liberating. For the different but no doubt salutary emphasis in the
Pastorals upon the Christian life as a life of discipline and training
cp., e.g., 2 Tim. 2:25; 3:16. We are not liberated by an act of divine
grace from *godless ways and worldly desires*, but trained to renounce
them, that is, to turn our back on them (ἀρνεῖσθαι, cp. 1 Tim. 5:8;
2 Tim. 2:12 f.). The *life of temperance, honesty, and godliness* is characteristic of the Christian ideal set forth in the Pastorals; cp., e.g.,
2 Tim. 1:7; Tit. 1:8; 1 Tim. 2:2. This kind of life is to be lived *in the
present age* (cp. 1 Tim. 6:17; 2 Tim. 4:10); there is another age to
bear in mind also (v. 13). It seems scarcely fair to say that our author
is un-Pauline here in his sharp distinction between the ages. The age
to come is not for him remote and insignificant; the life he requires
from Christians in the present age is possible only through the antici-
pation of the age to come in the work of Jesus (note that 'has dawned'
in v. 11 is the verb cognate with the noun 'appearing' which is used
of the return of Christ in v. 13; in some sense and measure, the age to
come has come). And, for *looking forward*, cp. Rom. 8:19, 23.

13   This verse is paraphrased in the translation. It would have been
better to retain the singular 'hope' (ἐλπίδα), for a Christian does not
have a number of 'hopes'; his hope is Christ (1 Tim. 1:1), as the
next words show. Certainly, hope here, with the adjective 'blessed'
(cp. 1 Tim. 1:11; 'God in his eternal felicity' = the blessed God),
is used in the sense of 'that which is hoped for', and notwithstanding
the Greek καί (and), it is meant that the hope will be fulfilled in 'the
appearing of the glory of . . .'. For the word 'appearing' (ἐπιφάνεια)
cp. 1 Tim. 6:14; it is used of a state appearance of a great monarch.

the splendour of our great God and Saviour[1] Christ Jesus
14 will appear. He it is who sacrificed himself for us, to set us
free from all wickedness and to make us a pure people marked
out for his own, eager to do good.

    [1] *Or* of the great God and our Saviour . . .

The author is certainly thinking of the *parousia* of Jesus Christ; hence
the rendering of the text, *of our great God and Saviour Christ Jesus*, is to
be preferred to that of the margin. Also in favour of this rendering
are (1) the fact that in Greek only one article is used, and (2) the
combined use in Hellenistic religion of 'God and Saviour'. Against
it is only the fact that it is seldom that New Testament writers directly
describe Christ as God. It is doubtful whether Paul does so (perhaps at
Rom. 9:5); but post-Pauline writers occasionally do so (e.g. John
1:1; Heb. 1:8), and the author of Titus is to be counted among them.
      From the second coming of Christ in glory we are brought back to
14 his earthly ministry and death. He *sacrificed* (literally, gave) *himself
for us, to set us free* (or, to ransom us) *from all wickedness*. The parallel
between this and Mark 10:45 (see also 1 Tim. 2:6) is especially clear
if the renderings in brackets are accepted. For the question whether
λυτροῦν retains the sense of payment (ransom) see note on 1 Tim. 2:6,
where a cognate word is used. Here the words are quoted from Ps.
130:8: 'He shall ransom (λυτρώσεται) Israel from all his wickednesses
(ἀνομιῶν)'. The meaning of this liberation is given in the positive
clause that follows; it is a release not so much from guilt, as from actual
sin, a cleansing and an impetus towards good works. For the latter
part of the verse cp. Ezek. 37:23 ('I will cleanse (καθαριῶ) them, and
they shall be my people, and I the Lord will be their God'), and
Exod. 19:5 ('You shall be a people marked out for my own (περιού-
σιος)'). This scarcely amounts to quotation; the author writes with
Old Testament language in his mind, for cleansing, and God's special
ownership of his people, are common Old Testament themes. For
eager to do good cp. 1 Pet. 3:13. It is doubtless correct that in this combination of Old Testament material with an echo of the gospel
tradition our author has presented the Christian message in a somewhat moralized form. It must, however, be remembered that he is
digressing here in order to present (in suitable form) the redemptive
truth upon which the moral requirements of the paragraph are
based, the 'indicative' of the Gospel which is the ground of the 'imperative' of the commandment. He is quite clear (3:7) that justification precedes the doing of good deeds (3:5); but equally clear
that the goal of justification is obedience.

15   These, then, are your themes; urge them and argue them.
      And speak with authority: let no one slight you.

3   Remind them to be submissive to the government and the

15   *These, then, are your themes* brings the section back to moral demand,
      by way of an injunction to Titus. The themes must be presented in
      ways suitable to the occasion: *Urge them* (cp. 1 Tim. 5:1; 6:2; 2 Tim.
      4:2; Tit. 1:9; 2:6—various translations) *and argue them* (cp. 1 Tim.
      5:20; 2 Tim. 4:2; Tit. 1:9, 13—various translations). *Speak with
      authority* (ἐπιταγή). This word is used differently at 1 Tim. 1:1; Tit.
      1:3. Here it presumably stands for ὡς ἐπιτάσσων, 'as if giving orders'.
      It is understood that this authority is qualified by the considerations
      given in 2 Tim. 2:24 ff. *Let no one slight you*: cp. 1 Tim. 4:12 and note.
      Titus also is assumed to be young (v. 7). One may suppose that
      there was, at the time and place of the writing of the Pastorals, a
      tendency not to pay due respect to the ministry.
           The last theme handled in this section is that of the attitude of the
      Christian to civil authority and to society. This is not a matter of
      which Christians are ignorant; they know the truth. But, here as
1   often, it is the necessary duty of the minister to *remind them* of what they
      know. *To be submissive*; cp. 1 Tim. 2:11; 3:4; Tit. 2:5, 9. The transla-
      tion in 2:5, 9 is perhaps preferable. Wives and slaves are not told
      submissively to obey their husbands and masters if they should com-
      mand them to do what is wrong, but to recognize the authority (which
      God himself has given) of those whose calling is different from their
      own. In the same way the Christian may and must recognize the
      (God-given) authority of the state, but without being submissive
      to it in a servile way.
           The government and the authorities either accepts the reading with καί
      (and), or paraphrases the awkward collocation 'rulers authorities'
      (ἀρχαῖς ἐξουσίαις; cp. Luke 12:11 for the use of these two words
      joined by 'and'). The asyndeton is probably best explained as due
      to the fact that the verse as a whole can be regarded as a list, which in
      fact contains in the Greek no 'and' at any point. Normally, of course,
      to recognize the authority of the powers God appoints is *to obey them*;
      so also in Rom. 13:1–7, with the special injunction to pay taxes. The
      use of πειθαρχεῖν, however, unlike that of ὑποτάσσεσθαι, probably does
      imply that the state was not at this time commanding (for example)
      the worship of the emperor. But the word has the sense of rendering
      obedience to duly constituted authority, an obedience to which a
      state that commanded idolatry might be said to have forfeited its
      right.

authorities, to obey them, and to be ready for any honour-
2 able form of work;[1] to slander no one, not to pick quarrels,
to show forbearance and a consistently gentle disposition towards all men.

3   For at one time we ourselves in our folly and obstinacy were
all astray. We were slaves to passions and pleasures of every

[1] *Or* ready always to do good.

To be ready for any honourable form of work in Greek recalls Rom. 13:3
('Continue to do right and you will have their approval'). This suggests
that the translation in the margin (*to be ready always to do good*) should
be preferred.
2   *To slander no one*: cp. 1 Tim. 6:4; 2 Tim. 2:24. The moral requirements laid upon the minister are in fact to be sought in all Christians.
To show forbearance is to be the opposite of quarrelsome; cp. 1 Tim. 3:3.
The thought is taken further in *a consistently gentle disposition towards
all men*, the advance being in the last words: the Christian must be
gentle not only towards his fellow-Christians, and not only towards
those who show gentleness to him. Cp. Matt. 5:43-48. This last
requirement forms an apt conclusion and summary of the section on
Christian obedience, which here comes to an end. The more detailed
precepts could all be regarded as applications of 'a consistently gentle
disposition towards all men'.

4. 3:3-11. SALVATION

The new way of life which has now been sketched is possible
not because man is of himself able (or even willing) to resolve
so to live, but because of the act of divine grace in Jesus Christ.
To this the author turns (v. 4), by way of reference to the moral
conversion of himself and of his readers (v. 3). The mode of
application and the consequences of salvation are mentioned in
vv. 5-8. A final warning against error, and those responsible
for it, follows (vv. 9 ff.).

3   *At one time we ourselves . . . were. . . .* Cp. 1 Cor. 6:11. Literally, the
first three statements are 'foolish, obstinate, going astray'; it is, however, right to put them together, as in the translation (. . . *in our folly and
obstinacy were all astray*) since they form a group. Those who had thus
thrown off God's yoke did not thereby become free, but entered upon
a degrading servitude, having as master *passions and pleasures of every
kind*. Hence their *days were passed in malice and envy*. The short descrip-

kind. Our days were passed in malice and envy; we were
4 odious ourselves and we hated one another. But when the
kindness and generosity of God our Saviour dawned upon
5 the world, then, not for any good deeds of our own, but

---

tion, which is too plain-spoken to require much comment, comes to a
climax with *we were odious ourselves and we hated one another*.

This lamentable state could be remedied only by divine action.
4 This divine action is described in v. 4 (cp. 2 : 11 for similar language and
thought); it consisted in the manifestation in action (*dawned*, $\epsilon\pi\epsilon\phi\acute{a}\nu\eta$,
suggests an epiphany, strictly an appearing, but the appearing
of a mighty and active person; see note on 1 Tim. 6 : 14) of the kindness
($\chi\rho\eta\sigma\tau\acute{o}\tau\eta s$) and *generosity* ($\phi\iota\lambda\alpha\nu\theta\rho\omega\pi\acute{\iota}\alpha$) *of God our Saviour* (probably
here God the Father; but cp. 2 : 13; 3 : 6). 'Generosity' is used in the
New Testament only here and at Acts 28 : 2 (the corresponding adverb
is used only at Acts 27 : 3), but it is a significant word in Hellenistic
(including Hellenistic Jewish) writers, who use it especially to describe the magnanimity of rulers (who sometimes at least were thought
of as divine). The thought here is of a sovereign Lord who makes
an act of unprompted and undeserved favour to his subjects, and does
so in a personal appearance. It is because God so acts that he becomes
our Saviour (this word also belongs to the religious-political vocabulary
of Hellenism). It follows immediately from what has been said that
God's act (since it arises from his own essential goodness) does not
5 depend on *any good deeds of our own* (literally, 'works in righteousness
which we ourselves have done'). This expression has a Pauline sound,
and conveys accurately enough Pauline doctrine; but 'righteousness'
($\delta\iota\kappa\alpha\iota\sigma\sigma\acute{v}\nu\eta$) is not used in exactly the Pauline sense ('works of law'
would have been the Pauline phrase), and faith, the Pauline counter-
part of works, is not mentioned. It is not unfair to say that faith, man's
confident self-abandonment to God's merciful activity, is implied; it
remains significant that it is not explicitly mentioned. The 'epiphany'
or 'dawning' of v. 4 refers to the once-for-all historic act of God in
Jesus Christ. Now that this has happened it becomes possible for the
divine activity to be applied directly to the individual person. This
does not happen on the ground of *any good deeds of our own* (this phrase
can be taken with *both* $\epsilon\pi\epsilon\phi\acute{a}\nu\eta$ 'dawned' *and* $\emph{\"e}\sigma\omega\sigma\epsilon\nu$ 'saved'), but
simply because God is *merciful* (for mercy see notes on 1 Tim. 1 : 2;
2 Tim, 1 : 16, 18), and in his mercy he has appointed a means of salvation: *he saved us*. It is clear from the context that here 'saved' refers
to the inward application to particular men of the universal act of
redemption. The appointed representative means is baptism: *the
water* (literally, and better, the washing, or bath) *of rebirth*, that is, the

because he was merciful, he saved us through the water of
6 rebirth and the renewing power of[1] the Holy Spirit. For he
sent down the Spirit upon us plentifully through Jesus Christ

[1] *Or* the water of rebirth and of renewal by . . .

---

washing which signifies and conveys the new Christian life. In the
genuine Pauline letters this is differently expressed. Through baptism
we are buried with Christ in order that as he was raised from the dead
in the splendour of the Father so we also might set our feet upon the
new path of life (Rom. 6:4); those who are baptized into Christ put on
Christ as a garment, and thus become one new person in him (Gal.
3:27 f.). The main Pauline theme in regard to baptism is that of death
and resurrection. That Paul means by this nothing substantially different from those New Testament writers who speak in terms of
regeneration (John 1:13; 3:5; James 1:18; 1 Pet. 1:3, 23; 1 John
2:29; 3:9; 4:7; 5:1, 4, 18) may be granted immediately; the difference in usage remains. It is, however, worthy of note that our author
uses not the language of John and Peter (γεννηθῆναι (ἄνωθεν);
ἀναγεννηθῆναι) but a word (παλιγγενεσία) of which the only other
New Testament use (Matt. 19:28) is eschatological. This points to
the fact (which is true also for John and Peter) that the new birth of
which the New Testament speaks is not a purely individualist matter,
but the incorporation of the individual into the work of kindness and
generosity which God is doing in the last days.

The connexion of the next words is ambiguous. The text of the
translation distinguishes two agencies in salvation: *the water of rebirth
and the renewing power of the Holy Spirit*. The margin speaks of one only:
the water of rebirth and of renewal (cp. Rom. 12:2) *by the Holy Spirit*.
Neither of these alternative renderings can be easily dismissed; the
latter may perhaps be preferred on the grounds that if the former had
been intended it would have been natural to repeat the preposition
'through' (διά). The matter is of some importance since if the former
rendering is accepted 'the renewing power of the Holy Spirit' becomes separable from baptism, so that some have seen here an allusion
to a rite of confirmation distinct from that of baptism; if the latter is
accepted, not only 'rebirth' but also 'renewal by the Holy Spirit' is
directly connected with baptism. This is in fact not only linguistically
but also theologically more probable, for it would be difficult to assign
distinct meanings to the rebirth and the renewal; rebirth is effected
by the Holy Spirit (cp. John 3:5). Not washing in itself, but the Holy
Spirit is the efficient cause in baptism (cp. Spicq, p. 288).

6   The Holy Spirit must not be thought of as an independent religious

7 our Saviour, so that, justified by his grace, we might in hope

---

agency. *He* (God our Saviour; v. 4) *sent down the Spirit upon us plenti-*
fully through Jesus Christ our Saviour. 'Sent down' is more accurately
rendered 'poured out' (ἐξέχεεν). It is important to note the word,
because it points back through Acts 2:17 (where it is translated 'pour
out') to Joel 2:28, the promise of the eschatological outpouring of
the Spirit, which was fulfilled on the ground of the death and resurrection of Jesus. Note also in this verse that both God the Father and
Jesus Christ are described as 'our Saviour' (cp. v. 4).

7   *So that.* The present translation, which breaks up the long sentence
beginning at v. 4, may suggest a false connexion of thought by these
words, which evidently make the purpose clause of v. 7 (so that, having been justified . . . we might become) dependent upon v. 6 (he sent
down the Spirit). But in the Greek, v. 6 is a relative clause expanding
v. 5 (. . . the Holy Spirit, *which* he sent down . . .). This relative clause
might be the main clause on which v. 7 depends, but need not; the
main verb could equally well be, and indeed probably is, 'he saved us'
(v. 5). The connexion of thought thus becomes: when God had
graciously and decisively acted on behalf of mankind through Jesus
Christ, in his mercy he saved us from our wretched and wicked
existence (v. 3) through baptism into a rich and renewing experience
of the Holy Spirit, in order that, having been justified, we might
become heirs. In this sequence of thought the author appears to stand
closer to Paul than is sometimes supposed, though he does not show
the precision and power of, for example, Rom. 5 and 6.

Justified by his grace. It is possible that the verb is not used here in
its Pauline sense of 'brought into right relations with God', but has a
more moralistic meaning (cp. perhaps Rom. 6:7). This would fit the
theme of salvation understood as moral conversion from the circumstances described in v. 3. There is, however, no need to conclude that
'justified' has this moralistic sense. The paragraph makes excellent
sense if we suppose that, after speaking of inwardly felt and morally
perceptible events, rebirth and spiritual renewal, the author returns
to consider, from a new angle, the objective event upon which all
these subjective events rest. In v. 4 this was described from God's
side; in v. 7 it is described from man's side. Through Jesus Christ God
has put men into right relations with himself, and constituted them
heirs to eternal life. For men as 'heirs' cp. in Paul Rom. 8:17; 1 Cor.
6:9; Gal. 3:29; 4:7; and elsewhere Heb. 6:12, 17; 9:15; James 2:5;
1 Pet. 1:4; 3:9. 'Eternal life' (cp. 1 Tim. 1:16 and note) is still in the
future; it is *in hope* that we look forward to it (cp. Rom. 8:23). 'He
had said that we have been saved through the mercy of God. But our
salvation is as yet hidden; and therefore he now says that we are heirs

8 **become heirs to eternal life. These are words you may trust.**

---

of life, not because we have arrived at the present possession of it, but because hope brings us to full and complete certainty of it' (Calvin). Our author is concerned in this paragraph to emphasize the present salvation of men from sin, but he loses sight neither of the origin of this process in God's historic act of redemption, nor of the fact that its issue must remain in this world a matter of hope. The ingredients of the Pauline doctrine of salvation are all of them (except faith, though this is implied; see above) present; but it must be repeated that they are not worked out with Paul's clarity of thought, or with his instinct for putting the right thing in the right place. We should not understand the Pastorals so well if we did not possess the other Pauline letters.

8   *These are words you may trust*; cp. 1 Tim. 1:15; 4:9; 2 Tim. 2:11. In these passages the formula is taken as an introduction to what follows; here our translation regards it as an appended comment on what precedes (cp. 1 Tim. 3:1 margin). This makes good sense; vv. 4–7 form a unit which the author must have regarded as embodying the substance of his Gospel, of which it may possibly be a quoted summary. This arrangement of the words is not, however, without difficulty. (1) There must be a presumption that here, as in the other passages, the 'faithful saying' follows the formula. (2) If we make a stop after the formula it is hard to deal with the following words (literally, 'and (καί) concerning these things I wish you to insist'). If these are to begin a new paragraph the καί (and) must be dropped altogether (as in the translation), or rendered 'also' ('Concerning these things *also* I wish . . .').

The stress upon the necessity for good moral behaviour is resumed. The translation detaches the purpose clause (ἵνα . . . φροντίζωσιν) from what precedes, and takes it as equivalent to an imperative: *Those who have come to believe in God* (i.e. Christians—'Our own people' in v. 14) *should see that . . .*. The rendering of the next words is uncertain (see margin). There is evidence in support of the view that the Greek verb used (προΐστασθαι) means 'to engage in an occupation'; hence, in conjunction with words (καλῶν ἔργων) which are literally translated 'good works', it may be rendered *engage in honourable occupations*. Against this rendering it may be argued (1) that the verb is at least equally likely to mean 'to take thought for, attend to', and (2) that 'good works' is a common expression (1 Tim. 5:10, 25; 6:18; Tit. 2:7, 14; 3:8, 14; cp. 1 Tim. 2:10; 3:1; 5:10; 2 Tim. 2:21; 3:17; Tit. 1:16; 3:1) which is likely to have its usual meaning. In view of these considerations we should perhaps prefer the marginal rendering, *to practise virtue*. Upon the decision reached here will

Such are the points I should wish you to insist on. Those
who have come to believe in God should see that they engage
in honourable occupations, which are not only honourable in
9 themselves, but also useful to their fellow-men.[1] But steer
clear of foolish speculations, genealogies, quarrels, and controversies over the Law; they are unprofitable and pointless.

[1] *Or* should make it their business to practise virtue. These precepts are
good in themselves and useful to society.

---

depend the way in which the following sentence is taken. Literally
this runs: 'These things are honourable ($\kappa\alpha\lambda\acute{a}$—the adjective used
above with "works") and profitable to men'. The text refers 'these
things' to the 'honourable occupations' just mentioned: they are
not only honourable in themselves, but also useful . . . . It would be possible
to stop at 'occupations' (or, with the margin, 'virtue'), and take
'these things' to mean 'these things that I am saying'. We should
then proceed as in the margin: *These precepts are good in themselves and
useful to society.* This rendering is not only possible but inevitable if we
accept the marginal translation of the first part of the verse. It seems
preferable too, for 'in themselves' is not in the Greek, and whereas the
marginal rendering makes sense without this phrase (and is perhaps
improved by its omission) that in the text scarcely does so (though
as the sentence stands it provides a false antecedent for 'their fellow-
men').

It is thus doubtful whether our Epistle enjoins Christians to seek
employment which is profitable to their fellows. Rather we see in
vv. 3–8 an example of a recurrent New Testament pattern: the de-
praved state of mankind apart from the Gospel; the divine act of
redemption, which takes place independently of men's desert; the
constant desire to do good which those who have put their trust in
God should feel, not with a view to earning his favour but in gratitude
for it.

The interpretation of v. 8c preferred above is reinforced by the
9 next verse: The precepts I give are good and useful ($\dot{\omega}\phi\acute{\epsilon}\lambda\iota\mu\alpha$); *but steer
clear of foolish speculations, genealogies, quarrels, and controversies over the
Law: they are unprofitable ($\dot{\alpha}\nu\omega\phi\epsilon\lambda\epsilon\hat{\iota}s$) and pointless.* For 'speculations'
cp. 1 Tim. 6:4; 2 Tim. 2:23; for 'genealogies' cp. 1 Tim. 1:4; for
'quarrels' cp. 1 Tim. 6:4; for 'controversies over the Law' cp.
2 Tim. 2:23; also 1 Tim. 1:7 ff.; Tit. 1:10 f., 14. We meet once more
the disputatious and factious opposition which again and again looms
up behind the Pastorals; it very probably reflects the speculations
and debates of Jewish gnosticism (see Introduction, pp. 13 f.).

10　A heretic should be warned once, and once again; after
11　that, have done with him, recognizing that a man of that sort
has a distorted mind and stands self-condemned in his sin.

12　When I send Artemas to you, or Tychicus, make haste to
join me at Nicopolis, for that is where I have determined to
13　spend the winter. Do your utmost to help Zenas the lawyer
and Apollos on their travels, and see that they are not short

---

10　This verse should probably follow immediately upon v. 9, without
paragraph division. The *heretic* is the sort of man who introduces
foolish speculations and quarrels, but the term used refers not so
much to incorrectness of theological opinion as to factiousness of
manner. He *should be warned once, and once again*; cp. Matt. 18:15 ff.,
a close parallel. If he neglects these warnings there is no more that
can be done for him: *have done with him*. This is not a technical term
for excommunication; in 1 Tim. 4:7; 2 Tim. 2:23 its object is error
(not the heretic); in 1 Tim. 5:11 its object is the younger widows,
who may be good women but must be rejected if they seek to be
placed on the roll of widows. The rendering 'avoid' would be too
weak, though this is included—Titus must not waste time and energy
in disputing with men whom patience (two warnings) has failed to
win over. The beginnings of an informal Church discipline (see
Introduction, p. 30) are to be seen here; there are circumstances
11　in which exclusion becomes necessary. *A man of that sort has a distorted
mind and stands self-condemned in his sin.*

5. 3:12–15. PERSONAL CONCLUSION

Vv. 12, 13 contribute nothing to the argument of the Epistle;
if the Epistle is pseudonymous they must be regarded as either a
fragment of a genuine Pauline letter, or as an attempt to add
verisimilitude to the pseudepigraph. V. 14 takes up v. 8; v. 15
is a concluding greeting in the usual form.

12, 13　For the personal notes see Introduction, pp. 10 ff. The situation
envisaged is that Titus is to be relieved in his duty by another of Paul's
assistants. *Artemas* is mentioned nowhere else in the New Testament;
for *Tychicus*, however, we may compare Acts 20:4; Eph. 6:21; Col.
4:7; 2 Tim. 4:12. On at least one occasion Tychicus, himself an
Asian, was sent by Paul into the province of Asia. If this verse does
not really belong to the context presupposed by the Epistle to Titus

as a whole the same mission might be intended here; but this is pure speculation.

Titus, when relieved, must join Paul in *Nicopolis*; most probably Nicopolis in Epirus, founded by Augustus to commemorate the naval victory of Actium, is intended. There Paul has *determined* (he is thus a free man, not in prison) *to spend the winter*. Travelling by sea was normally suspended (cp. Acts 27:9, 12), and travelling by land curtailed, during the winter months. It would be natural for Paul to

Nicopolis (Tit. 3:12; see the note). The sea is visible beyond the town.

confine his longer journeys to the summer, and to use the winter to consolidate work in an important centre; but it must be admitted that we have no definite evidence to prove that this was his regular practice, and 2 Cor. 11:25 f. suggests that he took risks.

It is important to note that Titus did not occupy such a position (as 'apostolic delegate' or the like) that he could not be replaced by other members of the Pauline circle.

13   *Help . . . on their travels*: cp. Acts 15:3; 20:38; 21:5; Rom. 15:24; 1 Cor. 16:6, 11; 2 Cor. 1:16; 3 John 6. This was an important service in the early Church.

Zenas the lawyer is not mentioned elsewhere in the New Testament. Elsewhere (Matt. 22:35; Luke 7:30; 10:25; 11:45 f., 52 f.; 14:3) the word 'lawyer' is used of experts in the *Jewish* law—scribes, or rabbis. In view of what is said in this Epistle (1:10, 14; cp. 1 Tim. 1:7 ff.) about Jews it is doubtful whether the word is used in this sense here;

14 of anything. And our own people must be taught to engage in
   honest employment to produce the necessities of life; they
   must not be unproductive.

15   All who are with me send you greetings. My greetings to
   those who are our friends in truth.[1] Grace be with you all!

   [1] *Or* our friends in the faith.

---

presumably therefore it must refer to a secular jurist. The word
(νομικός) was used in this sense in the Hellenistic age.

   Apollos may, but need not, be the well-known figure of Acts and
1 Corinthians: Acts 18:24; 19:1; 1 Cor. 1:12; 3:4ff., 22; 4:6; 16:12.

14   *See that they are not short of anything*, an instruction needing no
comment, and leading to the next verse: *Our own people must be
taught* (literally, 'let them learn'—i.e. the activity of teachers is not
necessarily implied) *to engage in honest employment* (cp. v. 8; a similar
marginal alternative would be possible here) *to produce the necessities
of life; they must not be unproductive*. The last clause should probably be
attached to the preceding: 'in order that they may not be unproductive'. The translation takes ἵνα to be imperatival, which is perhaps
unlikely. Productive (gainful) work was necessary in order to facili-
tate the Christian mission. V. 14 can scarcely be part of a genuine
fragment, but it probably accounts for the introduction of vv. 12 f.,
whatever their source may have been.

15   *All who are with me send you greetings.* Cp. 2 Tim. 4:21; also 1 Cor.
16:19 f.; 2 Cor. 13:12; Phil. 4:22.

   My greetings to those who are our friends in truth (literally, 'in faith',
ἐν πίστει; the translation in the text is better than that in the margin,
but invites confusion with 2 John 1; 3 John 1, where the Greek is
different). 'Our faithful friends' might convey better the double
sense, that the friends are Christians, and that they can be trusted.

   Grace be with you all! Cp. 1 Tim. 6:21; 2 Tim. 4:22. In the other
Epistles the plural pronoun is used; here it is strengthened by the
addition of 'all' (which in this Epistle is in the Greek, as well as in the
translation). Whatever the origin of these Epistles, it was certainly
expected that each would have many readers in addition to the single
persons to whom they are addressed.

INDEX[1]

[1] This short Index may be supplemented by the Table of Contents.